GrowBook

25 Steps to Mature Your Business in the Developing World

Updated & Expanded Second Edition

Evan Keller

with Jennifer Pettie, Mano De La Vega & Grace John

Creating Jobs Inc
DeLand, FL

*Grow*Book: 25 Steps to Mature Your Business in the Developing World, Updated & Expanded Second Edition

Copyright © 2020 by Creating Jobs Inc

All rights reserved. No parts of this book may be reproduced in any form without written permission from Creating Jobs Inc.

Published by:

Creating Jobs Inc

1702 N. Woodland Blvd #116437

DeLand FL 32720

World Wide Web: www.creatingjobs.org

E-mail: info@creatingjobs.org

ISBN-13: 978-1-7334519-4-9

Printed in the United States of America

*Dedicated to my precious wife of 28 years,
Karen Keller.
Thanks for always believing in me,
and being such an amazing example of selfless love.
You rock!*

P929 missing pic
162   "
213   29
                 160
                 212

Edit Graphics

226
24

Adjust on pg
✓19
✓55 Valores
✓79 Mejora
✓95 Estudio de Caso
✓101 Efesios
✓107 IS font?
✓111 Barreras up
~~118 Difund & Gree~~
~~119 Esti...~~
426

317 Identifique

Contents

Introduction 1

Part 1 | Leadership

Chapter 1 | Lead Yourself 15 13

Chapter 2 | Set the Course 47 39

Chapter 3 | Pursue Goals 65 55

Chapter 4 | Develop Systems 77 65

Chapter 5 | Innovate Constantly 93 79

Chapter 6 | Overcome Fatalism 111

Part 2 | Market Position

Chapter 7 | Craft Customer-Focused Branding 129

Chapter 8 | Generate a Sufficient Flow of Customers .. 147

Part 3 | Production

Chapter 9 | Create Unique Customer Solutions...........167

Chapter 10 | Produce Efficiently..................................179

Part 4 | Sales & Service

Chapter 11 | Close Sufficient High-Margin Sales 201

Chapter 12 | Multiply Happy Customers 217

Part 5 | Employees

Chapter 13 | Hire & Delegate to Leaders.....................237

Chapter 14 | Engage Employees 259

Chapter 15 | Build Teamwork......................................281

Part 6 | Finance

Chapter 16 | Achieve Positive Cash Flow....................301

Chapter 17 | Save Money Diligently............................315

Chapter 18 | Control Spending Closely.......................327

Chapter 19 | Negotiate Good Deals 347

Chapter 20 | Access Capital & Limit Debt 363

Chapter 21 | Manage Major Risks 381

Chapter 22 | Resist Corruption 397

Part 7 | Giving Back

Chapter 23 | Help Employees Grow 415

Chapter 24 | Mentor Other Entrepreneurs 433

Chapter 25 | Serve with Time, Talent & Treasure 451

Conclusion 467

Action Plan 473

Contributors 473

Bibliography 487

Introduction

By Evan Keller

DETOUR INTO BUSINESS:

What is at the confluence of Hurricane Katrina and Lyme disease? There began my detour into business – taking my life by storm. The hard-won advice in this book came from this unexpected stumble into entrepreneurship. A couple of months after volunteering in Mississippi – clearing Katrina-toppled trees off of homes and cars – my selfless wife of 13 years sat me down for a heart-to-heart that would alter the course of our lives forever. I was 34 years old and well into a seemingly lifelong career as a mid-level manager of a national nonprofit. Karen, a 39-year-old half-Japanese former nurse and the best cook I'd ever met, was in the fight of her life. She was nearly bedridden with Lyme disease. It had robbed six years from her, and the energy that rearing children would've required. (Also, her doctor had actually denied her an initial round of antibiotics after her tick bite that would have prevented the onset of Lyme altogether.)

2

THE HEART-TO-HEART THAT CHANGED EVERYTHING:

"Can we talk?" Her hushed yet earnest tone told me "this is big" as she pulled up a chair beside my desk in our cozy Central Florida home. "Since I'm not well enough to work any longer, your nonprofit salary isn't enough to pursue those expensive, alternative Lyme treatments that our insurance won't cover." Her brown eyes were weary with tears, yet steely with resolve. Karen is a fighter. "*I want to live again…..*What can we do?"

Karen was desperate, and her fight had to become my fight. I had to man-up and *do* something…but what? Her parents had both died young of lung cancer and she had no other family. I was her only safety net. So, I thought and prayed and…started a business four days later. I had no capital, no time, no business education, no expertise or experience in the industry I chose – except for that week of Katrina relief.

A SHAKY BUT **GUTSY** START:

But I *did* catch Karen's steely resolve. Little did I know that dogged determination is arguably the top trait an entrepreneur needs to slog through the years of adversity that precede success. So, I just went out and sold my smile, knocking on doors after my nonprofit job each day and all day Saturdays. I had no equipment, no insurance, no employees, and no business plan - just a failure-is-not-an-option drive to make it work. The first job I landed was removing two pine trees for an acquaintance I'd played hoops with at the YMCA. Given my inexperience, I agreed to do the job for half the going rate. His risk paid off as his fence remained unscathed. Little did he know that I'd looked up tree-felling techniques on the Internet the night before! Both of the borrowed chainsaws broke down on the job, and the borrowed 1979 Ford pickup got stuck in the mud when filled with pine logs. I thought I'd just start a little business and make a few dollars on the side. I soon found out that business consumes your whole life – extracting much before giving a little back.

BUSINESS **INSANITY**:

Stealing a rare hour away from the chaos of my life as a new entrepreneur, I slipped my kayak into the peaceful Wekiva River. But on the inside, there was a distinct lack of peace. Normally level headed, I was roiling with emotions that, as a man, I didn't know I had. My voice cut through the thick silence of that spring-fed waterway - "Help! I'm going to explode." If not for the word "explode," any paddlers in earshot would've connected that desperate shout to an attack from one of the many 10-foot gators lurking under the tannin-darkened waters. At that point, facing a single, simpleminded mouthful of teeth would've almost been preferred over the complex array of challenges that took chunks out of me all day, every day. My life was being pulled apart by the jaws of barely making payroll, customers who refused to pay for no reason, employees whose existence seemed hell-bent on my destruction, daily breakdowns of expensive heavy equipment, the constant whipping to and fro of the cell phone ring, the grind of 18-hour workdays, and job sites on which there were sundry ways to die. And this was after I had crew chiefs in place and no longer spent long days in the hot sun lugging logs, dragging brush piles and climbing trees. (One day my vision had blacked out from heat exhaustion atop a pine tree.) What had I gotten myself into?

BUSINESS SPITS YOU OUT A DIFFERENT PERSON:

Yet concurrent with all this chaos was a deep sense of satisfaction in this new venture I had birthed, the dozen jobs I had created and sustained in one of Florida's poorest counties, and the new sense of connectedness to (and corresponding influence in) my community. Having an art degree, I was surprised that business was such a fertile venue for creativity. I also marvelled at how business had changed *me*: I aged 10 years in the first three, developed pretty thick skin, and discovered some latent talents. My over-optimism had been tempered by a minute-by-minute duel with Murphy's Law. I'd learned about people: surprised by their immense kindness and thinly-veiled evil. I'd learned that bootstrapping forces you to be profitable from day one and provides a greater sense of accomplishment. How is business changing *you*?

This book shares what I learned about how to transform the chaos of a start-up into a well-oiled machine that serves everyone well – you, employees, and above all: customers. Learn from my mistakes, and perhaps make fewer of your own.

BUSINESS AS A FORCE FOR **GOOD**:

I was amazed by the good that entrepreneurs can do with their influence, profits, and skills. This, along with a passion to serve the poor that grew on eight Haiti and Katrina relief trips, led me to start a nonprofit to raise the capacity of developing-world entrepreneurs to meet the needs of their own communities. That's how I started working with my three co-authors: Mano De La Vega (below right), Jennifer Pettie (below left), and Grace John.

INTRODUCTION

Together, we "mentor and train entrepreneurs to grow companies, create jobs, and help communities thrive." In fact, much of the material in this book we've developed and taught to groups of business people in the US and abroad. We hope it helps you take your business further than you've dreamed. Maybe our hard-won advice will make your path a little easier. We hope that as your company grows, you'll use your expanding influence, acumen, and resources to make this world a better place. If you're interested in volunteering with us to empower other entrepreneurs domestically or internationally, check us out at CreatingJobs.org.

HOW TO USE GROWBOOK:

For an overview of leading your company to success, read GrowBook cover-to-cover. Better yet, read a chapter a month and begin implementing what you learn, powerfully accelerating your business over a two-year period. Or you could go straight to chapters you want to implement now. As you read, connect *Grow*Book to your business with the planning and application tools sprinkled throughout and at the end. Enjoy the book and let me know what you think: evan@creatingjobs.org. You may also be interested in the prequel: *Start*Book, which provides seven simple steps to launch a successful business (available on Amazon).

GrowBook Snapshot

GrowBook offers 25 steps to mature your business to operate smoothly and profitably – even when you're not present. It all starts with you setting goals to improve yourself and your business constantly, then taking steady action...

> Build a brand that centers on customer needs. Find a solution that customers crave and "wow" them every time. Give top-priority effort to turning that trust into a steady flow of new customers. To efficiently produce what your customers want, build a team of thriving employees who: share your values, have real responsibility, enjoy strong teamwork, and keep honing their skills. Give them a clear path to develop within your company. With your employees' help, build systems they can use to produce reliable and efficient results. Be frugal with spending and diligent with saving to patiently build financial strength. Use your expanding resources, acumen and influence to serve others.

The key pivot to putting GrowBook into practice is working less "in" your business and more "on" your business. Transition from being a great technician to a successful entrepreneur.

GrowBook
At-a-Glance

Figure out who you are and where you're going as a person and as a business. Improve yourself and your business every day, using reading, thinking, writing and acting as primary tools.

Center your marketing messages on customer needs. Until you have more customers than you can serve, make it your number one priority to find them online and face-to-face.

Provide solutions that customers crave and use customer feedback to improve them. Work to produce with ever-increasing efficiency.

Sell at a high margin based on trust and superior value. Reinforce both by exceeding customer expectations.

Multiply your capacity by raising up leaders with real authority. Create a win-win by helping employees grow their skills and build their teamwork. Show them a path for advancement, and that you care.

Steadily build wealth by being: vigilant in managing cash, diligent in saving, frugal with spending, strategic in negotiating, cautious with borrowing, and careful in protecting your business.

Use all you've been given to benefit others – serving employees, entrepreneurs, community and world. Therein your time, talent and treasure will find their true purpose and joy.

What does each aspect of my business need?
Write "maintain", "fine-tune", or "overhaul" under each icon.

My *BiG* Focus:

Figure out who you are and where you're going as a person and as a business. Improve yourself and your business every day, using reading, thinking, writing and acting as primary tools.

14

Chapter 1 | Lead Yourself

By Evan Keller

WHAT?

Definition

While the focus is naturally on leading your business, it all begins with leading yourself well. Too many organizations have collapsed along with its leader's personal life. Who you are, the quality of your relationships, how you spend your time, how you develop your mind, spirit, and body all contribute to your effectiveness as a business leader.

Expert Quote

"Spectacular achievement is always preceded by unspectacular preparation" (Zig Ziglar <u>Secrets of Closing the Sale</u>).

Assessment Questions (These 10 yes/no questions allow you to give yourself a percentage grade.)

1. Are you developing your mind and character?
2. Are you developing your leadership skills?
3. Is your pace and schedule sustainable over the long haul?
4. Are you organized?
5. Do you make productive use of time?
6. Do you have a regular rhythm of rest and reflection?
7. Are your down-time activities renewing for your mind and body?
8. Do you get adequate sleep, exercise, and nutrition?
9. Do you have a vision for your life outside of business?
10. Do you intentionally invest in your family and friends?

WHY?

Benefits

Health. If you take care of yourself, you'll have more to give your family and company.

Sustainability. You'll accomplish more in your company long-term if lead yourself well.

Fulfillment. Investing in yourself and others will bring you joy.

Barriers

Time orientation. Many cultures do not see time as a valuable asset to steward. Without intentionality, it will be hard for you to invest in your own growth while faithfully caring for your family and business.

Group orientation. Cultures which emphasis the group over the individual have many advantages, but a drawback is that it may seem selfish to invest in yourself. On the contrary, you'll have more to give to the group if you are committed to your own growth and health.

Limited Access. It will be harder to keep learning about leadership and business if such resources are not available in your language or location. Likewise, healthy foods may not be available.

Underlying Values

Character. Who you are is more important than what you accomplish. – Proverbs 28:6

Relationships. As a relational creature, your connections with others outrank your most important tasks. If you doubt this, ask yourself what you'd like said about you at your funeral. I don't you answered: "She worked so much that she never saw her family." In the end, life is all about relationships.

Trust. Demonstrating your reliability is paramount at home and work. – Proverbs 20:6-7

Investment. You can achieve more if you invest more in your own capacity and health. – Ecclesiastes 10:10

Balance. Work is a good thing, but it's not the *only* thing.

Humility. You are finite – you have limits. Honor them or they may destroy you.

Self-awareness. Develop your strengths. Do more of what you do best. – Romans 12:3

Stewardship. Your body, mind, money, time, and gifts are entrusted to you for wise use. – Matthew 25:14-30

HOW?

Steps to Implement

Leading yourself well requires investing heavily in these six areas of your life: relationships, character, time, body, mind, and money. Here are some first steps for each….

RELATIONSHIPS: Negotiate work-life balance with your family. This is my biggest weakness in leading myself since I'm addicted to creative problem solving in both of my ventures.

Karen is a patient woman! Check out this great INC Magazine article by Meg Cadoux Hirshberg: http://www.inc.com/magazine/201212/meg-cadoux-hirshberg/lets-talk-about-this.html (December 2012 edition, p.41-42). Hirshberg gives straight talk about her conversations with her entrepreneur husband. She offers 15 questions families can use to get on the same page.

RELATIONSHIPS: Keep your promises to family. If you have kids, be there for them. Marriages don't always work, but we give up too easily. It would help to have some moral integrity – be faithful to your spouse. The individual freedom we value so highly often sabotages our higher human calling to love unselfishly. Not only is divorce the leading cause of poverty in the US, it can also bring financial ruin to your business. Not the most popular things to say, but there you have it.

RELATIONSHIPS: Build strong friendships. Find people you enjoy and want to be like. Show them you care and value their friendships. Make time for conversations that connect at the soul level. Look for ways to emulate the traits you respect the most in them. Don't let the busyness of life crowd out these intimate friendships. Here are my favorite two ways to invest in them: doing meaningful work together in my non-profit and enjoying mountain adventures together. Both carve out meaningful time to do something joyful together.

RELATIONSHIPS: Build trusting relationships. "Too many leaders forget the basic law of influence: A leader can exercise influence only if people are willing to be influenced. Other than outright coercion, trust is the only way to create that willingness. No trust equals no influence equals no leadership" (Kent Lineback in "Leadership 2013: What Matters Most"). Another quote to drive home the necessity of building trust: "Trust is the foundation of all successful relationships. It is also the foundation of all successful organizations. Trust is not an entitlement but a virtue that is established over time. Our actions continually are evaluated by those we interact with to determine our level of trustworthiness....A primary role of leadership is to develop a high level of trust within the organization. Accordingly, the enduring success of an organization is built on the trustworthiness of its leaders....Customers strongly desire to do business with people they trust....A great way to earn trust is:

1. Do what you say.

2. Do it when you say you'll do it.

3. Do it right the first time.

4. Always under-promise and over-deliver.

(Kris Den Besten <u>Shine</u> p.61-62)

CHARACTER: Commit to constant growth. A national sales training expert made the audacious claim that "the ultimate path for business success is far more about improving yourself than it is about finding the right product, market or model." (David Kahle) Do you believe him? Similarly, Mark Miller writes: "Your capacity to grow determines your capacity to lead." (<u>Chess Not Checkers</u> p.43) That sums up this chapter in a single sentence!

CHARACTER: Grow your entrepreneurial traits. Some say you either have them or you don't. At the very least you can further develop the ones you have. As a business owner, you likely embody these already. The seven traits I feel you need most to succeed as an entrepreneur are: tenacity, optimism, risk acceptance, future focus, self-confidence, creativity, and nonconformity. Joe Robinson expounds on his similar top seven list in the January 2014 Entrepreneur Magazine article entitled "The Seven Traits of Successful Entrepreneurs" (p.48-49, http://www.entrepreneur.com/ article/230350). If you have room for more, Edpmindset.com has a list of 14. Feel free to rate yourself on my top 16 below.

How strong are my entrepreneurial traits?

Rate each trait from 1 (weak) to 5 (strong):

___ tenacious

___ optimistic

___ courageous

___ future-focused

___ self-confident

___ creative

___ non-conforming

___ problem-solving

___ action-oriented

___ self-controlled

___ hard-working

___ eager to learn

___ humble

___ servant-hearted

___ trustworthy

___ full of integrity

Average score: total score ___ divided by 16 = ___.

CHARACTER: Strengthen your character. What habits, vices, or negative character traits would you like to jettison? I'm working on being less critical and task-oriented (to the harm of my relationships). What virtues would you like to grow in? I'm seeking to better embody patience, gratitude, selflessness, and generosity. I've identified friends who embody these well. I'm watching them, emulating them, and asking how they came to grow in these character traits. You've heard it said that your potential is limited by the five people you spend the most time with. Character is the highest form of wealth – the true measure of your net worth. It's the most important thing about you.

CHARACTER: Pursue Transformation. It's one thing to *want* to grow in various character traits, but *how* do you actually cultivate such growth? I suspect the most profound answers to that question are found in the disciplines of spiritual formation which are beyond the scope of this book. Such growth is certainly not as simple as growing a tomato plant – just add soil, sun, water, and fertilizer. People don't change easily. It's a long and hard process like changing your physique through the discipline of diet and exercise. The habit of working out slowly builds muscle and leaves you looking different. Here's what a character-building workout looks like, according to David

Kahle: "Our character traits develop over time as the result of individual choices we make to think or act in certain ways. Our thoughts lead to our actions. Our actions, repeated, turn into habits. Habits harden into character traits. Character determines our destiny." So, however difficult, changing character *is* possible!

TIME: Make your business plan fit in with your life plan. Serial entrepreneur and INC Magazine columnist Norm Brodsky makes this the most important of his "Ten Commandments of Business": "The life plan has to come before the business plan." In his book, Street Smarts, he shares how his life "was one full-bore, supercharged, nonstop, 24/7 rush to create a $100 million business" while neglecting his family and his favorite activities. "Building a successful business is not an end in itself. It is a means to an end. It is a way to create a better life for you and those whom you love....You need to do the life plan first and then keep revisiting it, to make sure it's up to date and your business plan is helping you achieve it." I'm sometimes asked if my company is part of a national chain. I take that as a compliment to our branding, professionalism, and systems. I made the choice years ago *not* to go nationwide or to franchise because of my strong sense of calling to my nonprofit work. How will *you* make your business plan fit with your life plan – not vice versa? I hope your life plan is deeper than merely freeing up time and money. What will you do with that extra time and money? Why are you here? Write a brief personal mission statement that captures what you want your life to be about.

TIME: Delegate. Hire and train others to take on some of your roles. They may even do them better! This raises the capacity of your business – and its value as well. We have a hard time trusting, don't want to give up part of our "baby", think only we can do it, and enjoy the martyr complex of the extremely busy entrepreneur. But that mindset will prevent your "baby" from every growing up! That's not healthy for your business or sustainable for you. Who wants to change diapers forever? A *new* business is all-consuming, but if nothing's changed after five years, the problem is right there in the mirror! If you train others to wear some of your hats, you'll be able to better develop your leadership and focus on the big picture of growing your business. (See more on delegation in chapter 13.)

TIME: Organize your workflow. Find a system that allows you have a clean desk, quickly separate paper and emails into delete/do now/do later folders. Why? Because productivity comes from a clear mind. Five stages of managing workflow are: "We... 1. Collect things that command our attention, 2. Process what they mean and what to do about them, 3. Organize the results, 4. Review as options for what we chose to... 5. Do" (David Allen <u>Getting Things Done</u> p.24).

TIME: Organize your time. Prioritize big goals for your year/quarter/week and make sure these top priorities get big chunks of uninterrupted time. Don't let everyone else – especially via email and phone – dictate your priorities. It's not the number of things you cross off your "do list" that matters, but rather whether your top priorities got done with excellence. Do what you can to limit distractions so you can focus creative energy on what's important. "The key is not to prioritize what's on your schedule, but to schedule your priorities" (Steven Covey <u>Seven Habits of Highly Effective People</u> p.161). Covey drives this principle home with his "Time Management Matrix" – see below. Its four quadrants divide our uses of time by "urgency" and "importance." A key insight is that urgent matters scream "I am important" – but sometimes they lie! "We react to urgent matters. Important matters that are not urgent require more initiative, more proactivity" (p.151). He suggests we spend most of our time on tasks that are important-but-not-urgent, and severely limit activities that are not important. He points out that many crises can be prevented altogether by focusing on non-urgent-but-important work such as "relationship building, planning, exercising, preventative maintenance, and preparation" (p.154). Other good books advise you not to spend lots of time on things you're not good at, but rather to play to your strengths.

	Urgent	Not Urgent
Important	**I** Fire Fighting Crises Pressing problems Deadline-driven projects	**II** Quality Time Prevention, capability improvement Relationship building Recognizing new opportunities Planning, recreation
Not Important	**III** Distraction Interruptions, some callers Some mail, some reports Some meetings Proximate, pressing matters Popular activities	**IV** Time Wasting Trivia, busy work Some mail Some phone calls Time wasters Pleasant activities

TIME: Stop wasting it. Is your down-time truly renewing? Is your technology use out of control? Do you binge on Netflix?

What activities do you usually regret spending so much time on. Decide what you'll invest in instead.

BODY: Get moving. If you tie exercise to fun, it's more likely you'll do it. Whereas I'm addicted to sports and get lots of cardio, I'm in danger at middle age of starting to lose muscle mass. So, I'm forcing myself into weight training after a 30-year hiatus. Since a body-building friend told me, "the best workout is the one you'll do", I'm starting with a couple of daily sets of pull-ups, push-ups, and curls. Once the habit hardens, I hope to make the workout more substantial.

BODY: Get enough nutrition. Our food is killing us. Heart disease, cancer, and diabetes are *not* genetic. And they're all preventable. That's the storyline in Dr. Michael Greger's book How Not to Die, which is chockful of devastatingly convincing scientific research. Americans are overfed and undernourished. We eat for pleasure not nutrition, but we're strict about putting the right fuel in our cars. I've recently cut out 2/3 of the meat, dairy, sugar, and processed foods I'd been eating. I lost a dozen pounds in a few months. That's cool, but mostly I want to live healthier and longer. Here's a visual of a nutritious, whole foods, plant-based diet.

BODY: Get adequate sleep. A book called Brain Rules (bib) cites research that deep sleep helps you process what you learned during the day. People truly made better decisions after a good night's sleep. So, the old "let me sleep on it" saying is backed by science. I usually get eight hours and often wake up with good ideas before I get out of bed or finish my shower. In fact, I awoke from a deep sleep in 2015 with the concept and title for *Grow*Book. So, sleep is actually less about the body, and more about our next topic: the mind.

MIND: Create a rhythm of rest and reflection. Half a day weekly and a full day monthly may be good intervals for alone time to think and pray about your life. This habit will likely bring clarity to your calling, major decisions, and the ways you'd like to grow.

MIND: Get to know yourself better. Take assessments such as the Myers-Briggs, DISC, and especially StrengthsFinder to learn more about your personality, strengths and relational tendencies. Get feedback on the results from people who know you best. Use them to shape your approach to work and to better understand how you relate to people. "It is management of self that should occupy 50 percent of our time and the best of our ability" (Dee Hock, "The Art of Chaordic Leadership," Leader to Leader, Winter, 2000, p.22).

MIND: Hone your business and leadership skills. Read Entrepreneur and INC magazines. Learn through blogs and podcasts. Get certifications and continuing education for your industry, but focus on being a leader rather than a technician.

MIND: Stimulate your creativity. Grow intellectually through books and articles. Be a life-long learner. This will keep you sharp and benefit your business in unexpected ways. Reading sharpens the creative abilities of your mind, priming you to create unusually fitting solutions. Here's one recent example that happened to me....I was looking for ways to better live out our core values of "helping each other thrive" and "people over profits." I wanted to increase employee engagement and retention. This advice from Bo Burlingham's <u>Small Giants</u> got me thinking: "creating a culture of intimacy involves reminding people in *unexpected ways* how much the company cares about them....by *doing what most companies wouldn't dream of doing*" (p.112). That same evening, I read a Lausanne.org article which applies the following ancient agricultural metaphor from Deuteronomy to the modern business context: "Do not muzzle an ox as it treads out the grain." It pictures a working animal who wants to taste some of the grain it's helping to harvest.

The main application suggested by the article was to share the rewards of your business with your employees. So, I went to bed pondering, "how can I share the rewards of my company in unexpected ways by doing something other companies wouldn't dream of doing?" Then, suddenly, as soon as my head hit the pillow, it hit me! I'm building my wife a nice house this year and my brother bought a beautiful farm last year, so why can't we help our employees *buy a house!* Too excited to sleep, our new Mortgage Assistance Program began to take shape in my head. When finishing the "ox" article in the morning, I was struck by the fact that what confirmed to the Israelites that they were truly no longer slaves in Egypt was the fact that in the Promised Land, each family owned property. I took that as a confirmation that I was on the right track! To tie this story back to the connection between reading and creativity: nothing I read said to launch a mortgage assistance program. Rather, different things I read were ingredients stirred into my desire to embody our core values. Like dabs of different colored oil paints on the painter's palette, intellectual inputs enable us to bring new creations to life. So, read a lot to fuel your creativity. Mark Cuban does so – for three hours a day! And Warren Buffet devotes twice that much time to reading. Clearly, these billionaire entrepreneurs are on to something.

MONEY: Be wise with personal finances. Limit consumer debt. Spend less than you make. Build up 3-6 months of living expenses in case the business can't pay you for a stretch. Save diligently for retirement, perhaps in your company's SIMPLE IRA, which allows up to $12,500 of tax deferred savings per year. You and your business are like two ships lashed together at sea. If one goes under financially, the other likely goes with it. So, pay attention to the financial health of both ships.

If you make big investments in these six areas of your life, you'll be quite impressed with your future self! And in your ability to lead others well. Go for it.

Case Study

On my way to Haiti, I read these words of James Schall: "The real wealth of the universe is the human mind." (<u>On Christians and Prosperity</u>) Upon arrival, I met the proof of that claim. His name is Cadet Olmy. In his mid-twenties, Cadet is a married father of one who runs a tiny motorcycle parts store on a street corner in Léogâne (the epicentre of the January 2010 earthquake). The broad (and slightly crooked) smile that's a perfect match for his boyishly handsome face only occasionally displaces pursed lips and probing eyes. Those inquisitive eyes hint at the hungry mind which led him to ask me for French translations of all 62 sources in GrowBook's bibliography! (Alas, most are only in English. Who else even notices the bibliography?) He proceeds to mention some ways he's put his Haitian Creole edition of GrowBook into practice, such as, oddly, becoming a soccer coach since we wrote about the importance of a leader's health in this chapter.

His hunger to learn shows up even in his financial statements – the best I've seen in Haiti. He credits his Creating Jobs mentor (and my GrowBook co-author) Jennifer Pettie with coaching him on those. His long fingers, which mimic his wiry frame, hover over the records of income and expenses with the precision of a spider. In addition to the standard listings of "gross profit," "cost of goods sold," and the like, he had monthly totals of "lost sales" – the amount of additional revenue he'd have generated if he had all the motorcycle parts in stock that his moto-taxi-driving customers had asked for.

In an inventory-dependent industry such as his, he knows this is the biggest hindrance to growth. Cadet told us: "This business is not for me; it's for the customer. So, I must order the parts they want."

In his shoes, many would resign themselves to remaining a tiny business, bemoaning the lack of available credit. Our advice would have been to diligently record which parts customers request and reinvest a portion of weekly profits to slowly build up that inventory. But Cadet's voracious approach to learning helped to spark something far more inventive. What did he do? He started a...BANK! He did *what?* Yes, you read it right. He now collects savings deposits and uses some of that capital to grow his inventory. That's creating wealth straight from the human mind! When we marveled at his ingenious plan, he said: "All these ideas I found in the GrowBook." Rather than our chapter on innovation, I think he meant the spark that reading provides.

So, how does it work? Each of his 47 savings clients bring him small deposits either daily or weekly and can withdraw the total plus 3% interest after 6 months. This gives him a known amount to work with during a known timeframe. With his profit margin being greater than 3%, he can easily grow that capital by buying parts wholesale and selling them retail. As in all good transactions, everyone wins! His sales and profits are increasing, along with the pleasure of making his clients happier. The moto-taxi drivers have less down-time awaiting parts, thus can better take care of their families and passengers. Many of Cadet's savings clients are also moto-parts customers of his, and receive credit on parts up to the amount of their savings balance – earning them both interest and trust.

Speaking of trust, the fact that 47 people happily entrust their hard-earned money to a parts guy is remarkable! If he hadn't established a years-long reputation as a person of integrity, his fledgling bank would never have gotten off the ground. Character matters. So, to amend the quote we started with, it takes both ingenuity and trust to create wealth.

As half a dozen clients stop by to drop off small deposits, we are struck by how happy they are to give him their hard-earned money!

Cadet is helping them fund their dreams even as they fund his! As they giddily fork over 100 gourde bills, the banker seriously presides over the recording of the transactions with ink stamps and signatures. He returns their savings booklets (see below), whose front cover admonishes them with this quote from

GrowBook's chapter on Saving Money Diligently (in Creole): "Saving money is an important discipline that builds character." Cadet perfectly embodies this chapter's theme of growing in wisdom as a sure foundation for leading others and creating wealth.

Leading Self, Employees, Systems

SELF – Take an honest self-assessment. Seriously invest in your own growth.

EMPLOYEES – Your example may help them in their own personal and professional development.

SYSTEMS – Schedule regular retreat days, family days, and date nights.

NOW WHAT?

Summary

With business commanding so much attention, it takes intentionality to invest in yourself, your family and friends. Make time to read, recreate, and reflect. Take good care of your body and build strong, trusting relationships. Grow as a person and as a leader, with regular solo time to reflect on your own personal and professional development. Learn to leverage your time and workflow for productivity. You'll be a happier person and a better leader at work.

Application Questions

1. Please take above "How strong are my entrepreneurial traits" self-assessment. Better yet, ask your family, friends, and employees to rate you with blunt honesty!

2. Please take the "Investing in my…" self-assessment on page 35. Which self-investment will you focus on first and how?

3. What has sabotaged your previous efforts to lead yourself well? How will this time be different?

4. "What one thing could you do in your personal and professional life that, if you did on a regular basis, would make a tremendous positive difference in your life?" (from Steven Covey).

5. Whose trust do you need to earn and how?

6. What is your "life plan" or personal mission statement?

7. What workflow and time management changes do you want to make?

8. How often will you pause for rest and reflection?

1. Which needs increasing the most: sleep, exercise, or nutrition?

2. How many books do you want to read in the next 12 months?

Recommended Reading

<u>The Seven Habits of Highly Effective People</u> by Stephen Covey

Investing in my...

Relationships
Circle one: Maintain   Fine-tune   Overhaul

Character
Circle one: Maintain   Fine-tune   Overhaul

Time
Circle one: Maintain   Fine-tune   Overhaul

Body
Circle one: Maintain   Fine-tune   Overhaul

Mind
Circle one: Maintain   Fine-tune   Overhaul

Money
Circle one: Maintain   Fine-tune   Overhaul

Make it Happen!

What ideas has this chapter stirred in me?

What new light does this chapter shine on my leadership and my business?

What changes do I plan to make?

My actions to *Make it Happen!*	Completion dates	
	Proposed	Actual

Chapter 2 | Set the Course

By Evan Keller

WHAT?

Definition

Crafting and using foundational documents helps you lead your company in a single direction to achieve much over time. A vision statement paints the picture of the good future that will come from accomplishing your mission. A mission statement describes how your company will turn its vision into reality. Company values state what is important along the way, revealing parameters and distinctives. Together, these foundational documents should be used to define and direct your company.

Expert Quote

"'The fox knows many things, but the hedgehog knows one big thing,' wrote Isaiah Berlin. Your hedgehog combines your passion and your special talents with what you can make money doing" (Jim Collins in INC Magazine June 2012, p.71, based on his classic book <u>Good to Great</u>).

Assessment Questions

1. What one thing can you be best in the world at?
2. Are your existing foundational documents aligned with each other?
3. Do they express your highest hopes for your company?
4. Are they stated succinctly with powerful combinations of words?
5. Do you use them to lead your company forward?

WHY?

Benefits

Purpose. Well-conceived foundational documents tie daily work to a higher sense of purpose. Meeting this deep human need for meaning will increase job satisfaction and performance.

Identity. Foundational documents help define a company and may attract potential employees who resonate with them. However, employees may not stay if they discover that your company's *true* direction and values are inferior to those in writing.

Direction. Knowing your vision and mission helps you move steadily and purposefully toward a better future.

Achievement. Because people and companies have finite time and energy, they will accomplish more if they don't try to do too many things. Foundational documents give focus that can lead to remarkable success.

Barriers

Reactivity. Allowing the "tyranny of the urgent" to dictate your direction will yield only scattered short-term results.

Distractions. Crafting good foundational documents is hard work that requires time, creative energy, and good writing skills. Don't rush it; refine your drafts over a period of weeks since new insights will come when returning with fresh eyes.

Indecision. Some people don't know what direction they want their company to take. They feel pulled in many directions since they've not given serious reflection to their place in the market, to how their gifts and passions can best satisfy the world's needs.

Underlying Values

Centering. Defining what's most important makes it easier to say "yes" to what aligns and "no" to what does not. – Matthew 6:33

Focus. Going in a particular direction over the long-term is better than bouncing from one priority and strategy to another. – Philippians 3:13-14

Foresight. Lasting and worthwhile change often takes a long time to achieve. Vision is seeing the future that you want to turn into reality.

Strategy. Vision needs legs to walk out of your mind and into reality. Your mission describes the strategy you'll use to steer all the resources of your business toward your vision. – Proverbs 31:16

Ethics. The ruthless pursuit of goals which tramples people and the environment along the way undermines any virtue the goals may have possessed. Thus, written values provide parameters in which the mission can be advanced in good conscience. – Proverbs 11:1,3

HOW?

Steps to Implement

Write and brainstorm the big ideas for your vision and mission.

1. Make space and time to think (chapter 1).
2. Reflect on what your business can become the best in the world at.
3. Think about what you want to accomplish long-term and what actions will get you there.
4. Write a paragraph or bullet points about your vision.
1. Write a paragraph or bullet points about your mission.

5. Get feedback from people who know you well and whom you respect. Include mentors, partners, customers and employees if you have them. Specifically, ask them which of your vision and mission ideas will help you build a strong company. Record their input.

6. Simplify, condense, and focus. Don't try to say everything. The problem is that we fall in love with our own words. It's hard to cross out any of them! But, "when everything is important, nothing is important." (Traction p.68) Look for a key that if you acquire, it will unlock many other accomplishments you aspire to. This key is probably the hardest and most desirable achievement in your industry. I chose "Be the most trusted tree experts" as Tree Work Now's vision since trust is elusive in our shoddy industry. Yet, it is this core relational capital that creates so many positives that will make my business thrive: long-term relationships, focus on quality rather than price, increased demand, repeat business, and referrals. I chose "Grow strong leaders" as our mission because it is the key to earning that trust. If my employees are growing in responsibility, technical abilities, tree knowledge, character, and communication skills, they will naturally foster trusting relationships with our customers. So, by identifying the keys of trust and leadership, I am able to distil all my dreams for my

company in nine short words. That's what a good vision and mission are: powerful, memorable summaries that help you shape the future.

7. Now that you've identified key achievements and actions, shorten your paragraphs into statements. Decide on the one long-term vision you want to realize and the way you'll achieve it. Write each as single phrases or sentences. These are your first-draft vision and mission statements.

8. Shelf them completely, then revisit a week later with fresh eyes. Do this a couple of times and make minor revisions as needed. Remember that recent advances in brain science confirm the efficacy of the "sleep on it" maxim, so try reading your vision/mission draft before bed, think it over for a few minutes, then make revisions in the morning after it has percolated in your brain during sleep. It really works!

Craft a vision statement that is...

1. A vivid picture of the future written in present tense. We must see into the future and thus help to create it.

2. A challenging statement of what the outcome of your work will look like if you carry out your mission successfully. It should answer the question: "How will

the world be different when our mission is accomplished?"

3. Big enough to stretch you and your team, yet still possible given enough time and effort.

4. Focused on long-term results which will take 10-20 years to begin to realize.

5. The source of your company goals and plans.

6. Something your company can become the best at.

7. A picture of what you hope to achieve in your target market.

8. Tying your work to the common good. "How can we best serve?"

9. Moving your company toward solving an important problem or meeting true needs in the world.

10. Inspiring and motivating to you, employees, and customers.

11. Memorable and brief – able to be spoken in a single breath.

12. Revisited for possible revision every ten years, although the best vision statements will need little or no revision.

Craft a mission statement that…

1. States *who* does *what* for *whom* and *how*.
2. States the most important things you must consistently do to work towards your vision.
3. Forms the crux of your company strategy – how you will pursue your vision.
4. Pursues your vision in a way that aligns with your company values.
5. Is a single phrase or sentence which is "simple, clear, concise, unexpected, concrete, credible, emotive, and unique" (Made to Stick by Chip & Dan Heath).
6. Is measurable – has a tangible and possibly numeric aspect that relates to reaching your market.
7. Is revisited more frequently than your vision statement, perhaps every five years.

Differences between vision and mission statements:

1. While your vision defines the difference you want to make, your mission says how you'll do it.
2. While your vision is a picture of a successful future, your mission identifies the key strategies and actions your organization will take to move towards that vision.

3. While your vision is meant to inspire commitment, your mission directs action.

Craft a set of values that...

4. Defines the company culture you hope to build.

5. Shares expectations of your employees' character, attitude, teamwork, skills, and posture towards customers.

6. Reflects "why" you're pursuing your vision and mission. Your values unveil your deepest motivations for your work.

7. Expounds on your unique approach.

8. Reveals the most important parameters you want embodied.

9. Sets the ethical boundaries in which you'll pursue your vision and mission, such as concern for people and the environment. Values are an emphatic "no" to Machiavelli – the "means" matter as much as the "ends." You're committing to reach your goals in ways that do not violate values you deem important.

10. Is brief in order to emphasize your distinctives. Three to five values will harness the power of focus. If you have many more than that, group them by theme and sum up

each group with a powerful phrase. At Tree Work Now, we had 14 values that we felt were all important. To make them more memorable, useful, and easy to communicate, I grouped them as bullet points under the following five phrases. We value: "**wowing** customers, releasing teammates' **potential**, redeeming **team** conflict, **respecting** everyone, and **improving** constantly". The five words in bold further condense our values.

11. Are important tools in attracting and evaluating new hires. If an applicant doesn't share your core values, it's a bad fit. Period. Even if he/she has amazing talent, you'll regret the hire later.

Utilize these foundational documents in the following ways.

1. Make them an important part of your identity as a company, similar to a country's constitution. Then connect them to everything else by referring to them constantly: "The way Mykal rallied his team to complete this project was an amazing example of our core value of…" or "Our sales team moved us a lot closer to our vision by…"

2. Build your company culture around them. This doesn't happen automatically; a culture grows organically –

often contrary to the entrepreneur's intentions. "Culture drives a company. In the long run, the boss's most important job is to define and enforce it" (Norm Brodsky <u>Street Smarts</u> p.xiv).

3. Really live them. Otherwise they backfire, doing more harm than good. Authenticity is a high value in our culture today, so admit to employees when one of your company statements are more aspirational than actual: "We fall short in this area, but here is how we're inching forward. We need your help to get there."

4. Use them as a foundation when setting goals and making plans. Connect the dots for your employees, showing how both short- and long-term goals grow from your foundational documents.

5. Make personnel decisions with them. "You must hire, fire, review, reward, and recognize people based on these core values. This is how to build a thriving culture around them." (Wickman p.35) At Tree Work Now, a values mismatch disqualifies a job applicant even if their skills are a perfect fit. The first page of new policies we write explain how it aligns with our values. Each employee is rated in peer reviews on how well they've embodied our core values in the previous six months. We open many meetings with praise for people who've

recently lived out a core value particularly well. Gene Wickman tells of a company "that offered a weekly $20 gift card, albeit with a unique twist. The employee that received it the previous week would give it to the next employee who exhibited one of the company's core values. They had to email the entire organization and tell everyone who they gave it to and what core value that person exhibited" (Wickman p.76-77).

6. Test everything by them. Before introducing new products or services, borrowing money, opening another location, buying equipment, or hiring an employee, ask yourself: "Will this action align with our vision, mission, and values? Will this move us toward our vision or away from it?"

7. Use them to allocate resources. Direct the majority of your time, talent and energy towards advancing your vision and mission, in keeping with your values. Even good ideas can distract you from your central purpose. Jim Collins writes that "good is the enemy of great" (<u>Good to Great</u>, p.1).

8. Display them where employees and customers can see them – at your locations and in your documents. Tie them into everyday conversations.

Case Study

It often takes years for a new organization to settle on its identity and direction. Our nonprofit, Creating Jobs Inc, went through various foundational documents (and even organizational names) before settling on "Business for Global Good" as its vision (doubles as the tagline in our logo) and "mentor and train entrepreneurs to grow companies, create jobs, and help communities thrive" as its mission. Note how the vision is brief, broad, and paints a big picture of the future. The mission shows how we hope to bring the vision to fruition. It outlines our top two strategic actions to reach our three main objectives. While the vision provides an inspiring end, the mission details our strategy to get there. Our four values further reveal our distinctive approach. Together, it is easy to measure any potential goal or initiative to see if it aligns with these foundational documents.

Leading Self, Employees, Systems

SELF – This is among the most important and far-reaching work you'll do in your business. Give it all the time and reflection that is necessary. Remember to make sure your business plan serves your life plan, as discussed in the previous chapter.

EMPLOYEES – Involve employees in the process of honing these documents. While *you* need to guide the ideas, get input on the most potent wordings from your employees. "If you want to go quickly, go alone. If you want to go far, go together." (African Friends and Money Matter, p.65, by David Maranz, SIL International 2015).

SYSTEMS – Goal-setting worksheets can have your vision, mission, and values embedded into them, encouraging your team to write long- and short-term goals that embody them. You can build other processes to develop, communicate, and build ownership around your foundational documents.

NOW WHAT?

Summary

Honing your vision, mission, and values sharpens focus on who you want to become and what you hope to accomplish as a company. When well-written and well-utilized, they will inspire and move your team in a single direction. Everything from goals to products, company culture to strategic initiatives, should flow from and remain true to these foundational documents.

Application Questions

1. Will you keep, revise, or replace your existing foundational documents?
2. Do you understand the differences and synergy between your vision, mission, and values?
3. Which key people inside and outside the company will you involve in the process?
4. When will you carve out time to work on this?
5. How many weeks will you contemplate your documents before finalizing them?
6. How will you communicate them and work them into your company culture?
7. How will you use them to drive company initiatives?
8. How will these internal identity pieces relate to your external branding? (See chapter 6).
9. Do you need to improve your writing skills? (See below).

Recommended Reading

<u>Good to Great</u> by Jim Collins

<u>Writing Tools</u> by Roy Peter Clark

<u>Made to Stick</u> by Chip & Dan Heath

Make it Happen!

What ideas has this chapter stirred in me?

What new light does this chapter shine on my leadership and my business?

What changes do I plan to make?

My actions to *Make it Happen!*	Completion dates	
	Proposed	Actual

Chapter 3 | Pursue Goals

By Evan Keller

WHAT?

Definition

Setting and achieving goals for the year can be the biggest catalyst to growing your business and making progress towards your long-term vision and strategy.

Expert Quote

"'Begin with the end in mind' is based on the principle that all things are created twice. There's a mental or first creation, and a physical or second creation to all things." – Stephen Covey, p.99 <u>The Seven Habits of Highly Effective People</u>.

Assessment Questions

1. What barriers, such as a short-term survival mentality, keep you from setting goals?

2. What derails you from achieving goals – not setting the right ones or not working on them consistently?

3. What are your top goals for the year? Do your employees know what they are?

4. Do your short- and long-term goals tie into your vision, mission, and values?

5. How often do you consult your goals and discuss progress towards them with your employees?

WHY?

Benefits

Focus. Building a successful company requires focused effort over a long period of time. Goals help to set and maintain that focus.

Direction. Effective leaders know where they're going. Without this discipline of "self-leadership," entrepreneurs cannot communicate a clear picture of where their company is headed. Use company goals to get your employees all working in the same direction as a team.

Discernment. Identifying in advance what is truly important helps you navigate the chaotic circumstances that you face daily in business. Goals help you be "proactive" rather than "reactive." If you don't work consciously from your goals, you find yourself simply "putting out fires" all day rather than intentionally leading in a certain direction. A focus on goals helps you discern between what is merely "urgent" and what is truly "important." So instead of wandering aimlessly, you can steadily and purposefully move your businesses toward your vision.

Productivity. Goals help to harness time for productivity. We all have the *same* 24 hours per day to be good stewards of. "You cannot buy, bank, or borrow even a second more, but you *can* use the time you do have wisely." – Larry McGehe (overheard training entrepreneurs in Honduras).

Barriers

Lack of hope. Who plans for a future they believe is dark and beyond their influence? Positivity drives planning.

Lack of vision. If your company vision and strategy lack clarity or focus, it will be hard to plan ways to advance them.

Lack of margin. If your company depends too much on you for its operations, you won't have time or creative energy to set the course into the future.

Lack of strategy. Many entrepreneurs are stoked by the big vision, but lose steam in the daily grind of detailed implementation. Some don't know which incremental steps could lead to realizing their big vision. Know yourself and lean on others who complement you.

Underlying Values

"If you aim at nothing, you'll hit it every time." If you're not pushing forward, you're drifting backward.

"Rome wasn't built in a day." Don't be discouraged if success is far off. Big wins take time.

"Take the bull by the horns." Tackle your biggest obstacle with direct, fearless initiative. – Proverbs 14:4

"Carpe diem" translated as "seize the day." Take initiative to make it happen while "opportunity knocks" (Roman poet Horace).

"Ants are creatures of little strength, yet they store up their food in the summer" (Proverbs 30:25). Planning ahead is wise.

"Good planning and hard work lead to prosperity, but hasty shortcuts lead to poverty" (Proverbs 21:5). Careful planning pays off.

HOW?

Steps to Implement

Make time to think. Reflecting on the future of your business is among the most important things you can do with your time. It is truly working "on" verses "in" your business.

Write your goals down. This brings focus to your thoughts, and makes your goals more "real." "Writing is hard copy thinking." – Dr. Carol Keller-Vlangas (as told to author).

Share your goals with your employees, especially since you need their help! Get employee input on your goals. Delegate responsibility appropriately and provide whatever support will help them be effective. Celebrate accomplished goals together!

Connect goals to your long-term vision. Begin your goal-setting session by reflecting on your vision, mission and values. This anchors your goals to what is most important to your business, giving them purpose and motivating you to achieve them. Start by setting three-year goals, then backtrack to one-year and 90-day goals. This bridges the present to the future.

Craft goals in response to a SWOT analysis. Looking at your strengths, weaknesses, opportunities, and threats, consider questions such as: what inefficiencies do you need to correct? What employee issues and gaps need addressing? What changes in the market must you adjust for? What is the bottleneck in your production? How can you better attract and "wow" customers? What capital improvements will raise your capacity?

You may want to craft goals in each of the seven categories of business management identified in this book (using the Big Picture). The Action Plan (also at end of the book) will help you identify which of *Grow*Book's 24 chapters to set goals for.

Make your goals specific and measurable. A good goal is concrete enough that everyone can plainly see whether it's been completed or not. If necessary, break conceptual or complex goals down into small action steps that can be tackled individually. Think big; start small.

Assign a timeframe to complete each goal. This encourages a sense of urgency.

Prioritize your goals. This ensures your most important ones get the focus they deserve.

Track goals regularly. Post them where you will see them often, and refer to them in your work every week. Track your progress once a month.

Repeat. Adjust your goals every quarter, with longer term goal setting once a year.

Case Study

I crafted a pageful of goals to complete within three years – then I ditched them. Why? Reading about employee engagement convinced me that "weigh-in is buy-in." If my leadership team helps to shape goals, they'll help to accomplish them. I did provide some direction by crafting four permanent core objectives that grow out of our vision, mission, and values.

Then I asked our leadership team: "What in our DNA (vision, mission, values) relates to these core objectives?" After showing how the objectives grow out of our DNA, we began the process of creating one main goal under each objective, complete with 90-day key performance indicators to measure our progress. This is a much longer process than simply cranking out goals on my own. But it's worth it if I'm not pursuing goals on my own.

Leading Self, Employees, Systems

SELF – Have you delegated enough responsibility so that you have some margin to focus on the big picture? Do you know what your most important priority for this quarter should be? Be a good model to your employees by making steady progress on the goals you're responsible to complete.

EMPLOYEES – They need to know where they're going, which also gives you a basis for accountability and reward. There may be some goals (personnel or financial) that you may want to keep to yourself.

SYSTEMS – Written goals are systems if you have a process to pursue them. Coupling goals with the calendar – another system – multiplies their impact and immediacy. Implementing a regular schedule of reviewing and revising plans will make the difference between good intentions quickly forgotten and positive change integrated into your company culture.

NOW WHAT?

Summary

With input from key employees, take significant time to write goals for the year based on your long-term vision and strategy, and then pursue them every month with focused, undaunted effort.

Application Questions

1. Can you set aside a day each quarter to reflect on the direction of your company?

2. What can you do this year to move towards your long-term vision and strategy? What smaller goals can be tackled in the next 90 days?

3. Which of the 24 steps in this book would you like to master in the next twelve months? (See the Action Plan, a goal setting tool at the end of the book.)

4. How will you keep yourself and your team on track with pursuing goals throughout the year?

5. How can you better align your business, personal, spiritual, financial, health, and family goals?

Recommended Reading

SMART Goals: wikipedia.org/wiki/SMART_criteria

Make it Happen!

What ideas has this chapter stirred in me?

What new light does this chapter shine on my leadership and my business?

What changes do I plan to make?

My actions to *Make it Happen!*	Completion dates	
	Proposed	Actual

Chapter 4 | Develop Systems

By Evan Keller

WHAT?

Definition

A system is a specified way of doing things. It shows your employees "how we do it here." You can develop systems by finding the best way to do things and repeating the process the same way each time to improve efficiency. Systems work best when you record them step-by-step so employees can implement them without a drop in quality or productivity. Doing things in a predictable, uniform way produces more reliable results.

Expert Quote

"Good documentation designates the purpose of the work, specifies the steps needed to be taken while doing that work and summarizes the standards associated with both the process and the result" (Michael Gerber <u>E-Myth Mastery</u>).

Assessment Questions

1. Do you work for your business or does your business work for you?
2. Which aspects of your business depend entirely on you?
3. What keeps you from documenting your systems and using them in your daily operations?

WHY?

Benefits to Employees:

Structure. Systems contribute to order which builds confidence in employees. "Documentation says, 'This is how we do it here.' It provides your people with the structure they need and with a written account of how to get the job done in the most efficient and effective way" (Michael Gerber <u>E-Myth Revisited</u> p.104).

Clear Expectations. Having clear job expectations is an important need for employees, and documented systems help fulfil that need. Knowing what is expected of them provides a sense of security as they do their job well.

Safety. Systems can improve safety by including precautionary steps and making outcomes more predictable.

Benefits to Production:

Quality. Reliable quality will increase as a system is adhered to and continuously refined.

Increased Capacity. Systems pave the way for growth. But if you insist on doing everything yourself, your business will remain small. If you delegate work without proper systems in place, your business will be too inefficient to grow. But if you continually develop more systems and train employees to use them, you can successfully delegate more functions of your business. This is what working "on" your business, instead of "in" your business, is all about.

Less People-dependent. Is your business people-dependent or systems-dependent? McDonald's has 28,000 stores and has the same food in each…amazing! Their system runs the business and their people run the system. McDonald's isn't known for having the most talented people; they don't have to have the best and brightest because they have an awesome system which breaks complex tasks down into manageable steps. Michael Gerber says that systems "help ordinary people produce extraordinary results."

Benefits to Customers:

Predictability. Systems increase predictability which builds trust with clients. "A good system guarantees the customer that her expectations will be fulfilled in exactly the same way every time" (Michael Gerber).

Trust. Doing what you say you'll do demonstrates your integrity which makes people want to do business with you. Delivering consistent results creates happy customers.

Benefits to entrepreneur:

Profit. As systems help every part of your business improve in productivity, increased profits should result.

Training Tools. When written, explained and modelled, systems can be used to train employees. Compile them into an operations manual.

Consistent Supervision. If two employees are consistently late to work, but they are not treated equally, it will cause dissention among them. If you have a tardiness policy and enforce it consistently with all employees, they'll know they are treated equally. You also may have less tardiness and they'll know you mean what you say.

Virtual Managers. When you're running a small company, you often wish you had another you! Good systems are probably the next best thing. Systems act as managers for you since they help enforce how you want things done – especially when you're not around. You can keep employees accountable to following systems by requiring a signature each time they go through the process, as well as discussing adherence to systems in supervisory conversations.

Time Savings. Systems save you time when doing occasional tasks. You don't have to reinvent the wheel when doing something you haven't done in a while. For example, if you haven't hired anyone for a year, but wrote down good interview questions last time, then you can begin the process quickly. If you have written down items to train new employees in, it gives you a head start the next time you hire someone.

Free Your Mind. Systems free your mind to do creative thinking in other aspects of your business.

Free Your Time. Good systems can also free you up for time with your family and time to serve in your community.

Business Valuation. No one wants to buy a business that they'll have to run on their own. If there are clear, effective systems in place implemented by strong leaders, you have a gold mine if you ever decide to sell it.

Barriers

Lack of time. Putting your systems down in writing is hard work because it requires thinking, focus, creativity, and time.

Resistance to change. It's natural for employees and entrepreneurs to resist change, even when it's clearly necessary.

New way of thinking. It can be hard to identify the steps in a familiar process you do all the time. You can make an audio recording of how you run a particular process in your business, then write down the steps as you listen to it.

Underlying Values

Efficiency. Employees don't care about your business as much as you do, but your systems can help them produce efficiently without putting as much thought into it as you have. – Proverbs 22:29

Quality. If used correctly, systems can maintain your standard of excellence. – Mark 7:37

Order. Employees and customers value this. – I Corinthians 14:33

Reliability. Customers want a predictable experience.

Innovation. It's easier to analyze and improve it when a system is written in steps on paper.

Discipline. Defining repeatable processes is painstaking work. – 2 Thessalonians 3:8

HOW?

Steps to Implement

Identify your existing systems. Everyone relies on systems in their daily lives, such as any routine you do automatically in roughly the same way on a regular basis, like getting dressed or driving a car. "I could do that in my sleep" refers to systems embedded in your routine. You already have such systems in your business as well, even if you just get things done with unwritten processes. I encourage you to identify them, write them down, improve them, and use them to train and supervise your employees to do their work properly.

Choose the right type of system. The process you're designing may be better suited as a recipe, schedule, database, policy, how-to guide, contract, diagram, chart, table, checklist or form.

Break into steps. Identify something that should be done over and over in your business. Break the task into steps and write them down as a guide. Identify the what, where, when, why, how. Specify standards to achieve the level of quality you desire.

Try it. Test a trial version of your system for a short period of time with a limited audience. Some improvements will become obvious.

Improve your systems. Just having systems isn't good enough. There are lots of systems that don't work. Can we be honest? Because they can tax instead of having to please customers, governments all over the world have poor systems. Inefficient systems can actually slow processes down and make them harder – the "red tape" of government has likely already come painfully to mind, complete with many "hoops to jump through." On the other hand, good systems are efficient, completing processes in as few simple steps as possible while treating people with dignity. They are implemented by the right people at the correct interval, and are used to increase quality and efficiency. Use your systems to train employees and keep them accountable. Get ongoing input on their effectiveness from the people implementing your systems and the people your systems are serving. Use feedback from both employees and customers to improve systems on a regular basis, perhaps four times a year.

Establish a timeframe for each step. A well-designed system that is carried out too slowly is still a failure. Set goals for speeding up your sluggish systems.

Train and supervise their use. Give copies of the written system to your employees, communicating why and how. You may want them to chart their completion of the steps, such as cleaning of a bathroom, pre-trip inspection of a truck, or dispensing of medicine to a pharmacy customer. Using the step-by-step guide you've created, train your employees to put it into practice. Show them how, then supervise them as they follow the steps to ensure it is producing the results you want.

Consider what systems you need to build in these categories:

1. **Lead generation and sales** – process to follow up leads, program to increase recurring sales program, cross-selling process, referral program, lead source tracking, and lead conversion tracking.

2. **Customers** – product catalog, process for clear communication before and during sale, timeline/script to thank and ensure satisfaction after the sale, process to address problems and complaints, and regular follow up with major clients.

3. **Employees** – job application, hiring process, job descriptions, training procedures, substance abuse policy, attendance policy, employee handbook, and processes for accessing various benefits. Having "standard operating procedures" posted where they can use them are good steps to putting them into practice.

4. **Maintenance of facilities and machinery** – checklists for: maintaining equipment, opening and closing a store/office, and cleaning of bathrooms, showrooms, and kitchens. Make a chart and have employees initial when complete.

5. **Production** – division of labor, workflow design, assembly instructions, recipes, safety procedures, purchasing and inventory management, production guide for each product, and shipping process. For more, see chapter 10.

6. **Finance** – profit and loss statement, balance sheet, cash flow statement, tracking efficiency ratios important to your business, and processes for collecting and storing records and tax documents.

7. **Time** – use a calendar to mark weekly, monthly, quarterly and yearly tasks that you need to do but may forget to do. This won't help unless you make the habit of looking at the calendar every day.

Case Study

Because good people and good systems are in place in my business, I'm able to devote 60% of my time to running my nonprofit, Creating Jobs Inc. While I love my company, my deeper passion is helping others leverage "business for global good." If there weren't good processes in my business, there's no way I could've written this book, which is a system in itself. Here is an example of one of our systems at Tree Work Now, our Lead Entry & Follow Up Policy:

For those who fit our customer profile, we communicate with ALL promptly, but set different timeline expectations for size of job and distance to job, as follows:

a. The targets for emergency jobs are: immediate lead entry, service same day or next morning if after dark.

b. The targets for larger and closer jobs are: estimate scheduled within 2 business days (but ASAP), estimate given within 5 days, and job completed within 10 days.

c. The targets for smaller and distant jobs are: first phone contact within 2 business days, estimate given within 10 days and job completed within 20 days.

    d. Post-hurricane targets are: first phone contact within 5 business days, estimate given within 15 days and job completed within 25 days, with more frequent communication while they wait.

    e. If we cannot fulfill the above expectations, we call each customer to realign expectations.

Note that whereas smaller and distant jobs are assigned longer timeframes, these guidelines ensure that every customer receives prompt communication and reliable follow through.

Leading Self, Employees, Systems

SELF – Creating systems is a very smart use of your time. There's something about creating words that help you recreate the physical realities they refer to. Amazing.

EMPLOYEES – Ask those who know certain processes to document them for review with you. Be sure you frame systems as dynamic tools that they can help you refine. Far from boxing them in, systems can free them to focus creative energy on new challenges.

SYSTEMS – How to lead systems on systems? Redundant! But seriously, you may want to put a timeline together to prioritize your development of needed systems over the next year.

NOW WHAT?

Summary

A system is a step-by-step process that you follow to complete a particular task so that you get a specific outcome. Instead of reinventing the wheel each time you must do something, you have a written checklist of steps that you or your employees can follow to complete the task "your way". By creating systems, you can easily teach someone else how to do what you do, then delegate the tasks so you have more time to focus on things only you can do. This increases efficiency in your production and provides a more consistent experience for your customers. Given the multitude of above-cited benefits to employees, customers, production, and entrepreneurs, it's a wonder that many still run their businesses "by the seat of their pants," never getting out of crisis mode. It certainly isn't easy, but defining repeatable processes is essential when expanding your workforce, opening a new location, or franchising. So, I encourage you to identify the systems you already have, create new ones, then compile, use, and refine them.

Application Questions

1. What systems do you have already? How have they helped your business? How good are they? Do you need to improve them or train your employees to use them?

2. What systems do you need to add? Which one will you develop first?

3. Which of the follow categories do you need to build systems in: lead generation, sales, production, employee management, finance, time, maintenance of facilities and equipment?

Recommended Reading

E-Myth Mastery by Michael Gerber

Make it Happen!

What ideas has this chapter stirred in me?

What new light does this chapter shine on my leadership and my business?

What changes do I plan to make?

My actions to *Make it Happen!*	Completion dates	
	Proposed	Actual

Chapter 5 | Innovate Constantly

By Evan Keller

WHAT?

Definition

The best business owners are energized by the challenge of making their businesses better every day. This culture of constant innovation applies to everything from products to processes to customer experience and needs buy-in from employees. Always improving is key to providing better solutions for customers and improving your competitive position.

Expert Quote

"Creativity is the only viable source of change" (<u>Culture Making</u> by Andy Crouch p.73).

Assessment Questions

1. What was the most exciting period in the history of your business and why?

2. What are the best changes you've made in your business? What prompted you to make these changes? How did you manage the changes and the disruptions they caused? Was it worth it?

3. What barriers keep you from making improvements you know you should make in your business?

WHY?

Benefits

Profit. Providing innovative solutions for clients will increase your revenue. Creative cost savings will increase your profit margin.

Joy. Since creativity and appreciation for excellence are integral to our humanity, we gain satisfaction in finding creative ways to make things better. We feel most alive when we're using our minds to improve ways of doing things, designing or improving products, and finding better ways to satisfy our customers. While resisting change leads to boredom, striving for steady improvement keeps us engaged. A job well done is a reward in itself.

Business Health. A stagnant business is in decline. A river should be flowing, a child should be growing. An improving business is a healthy business.

Client Fulfilment. Customers' needs and wants change over time, and if we don't adapt, we will be left behind. Market demands shift with consumer tastes and trends, and we need to stay aware of them. Even if our core product doesn't change much, its packaging may need updating, its marketing message may need to shift, and its customer service should adjust to new expectations.

Competitive Edge. Use competition to keep yourself sharp! Having competitors proves that people really want your product or service. Instead of fearing competition, use it to push yourself to innovate. Pay attention to what your competitors are doing; learn from their successes and failures. Competition is good for clients too, giving them the best value at the best price.

Industry Improvement. As you steadily provide better value to your customers, your market share grows and competitors must also improve to stay in business. Over time, your innovations help to raise the standard for your industry as a whole.

Barriers

Fear. If you're not experiencing small failures regularly, you're playing it too safe. After facing their fears and finding initial success, some business owners stop taking risks. No risk, no reward.

Resistance. Never say "this is how we've always done it." If your business hasn't changed much in the last year, something is wrong! Don't be satisfied. Be passionate about getting better every day.

Boredom. If you're creative energy has moved on to something else, it might be time to sell your business.

Pessimism. You cannot lead positive change without confidence and hope for a better future.

Technician mindset. If you're consumed with daily operational demands, you have little time for creativity. To be a leader, you must make significant time and space to ponder creative solutions and future growth.

Not learning. Constantly soak up great ideas from experts in person and in print, and from your employees and customers.

Underlying Values

Creativity. Its core to who we are as humans. – Geneses 2:19-20

Stewardship. We need to use our gifts for good. – Geneses 2:15

Courage. Risk brings reward.

Optimism. We *can* make a difference. – 2 Thessalonians 1:11

Diligence. Work is good. – Proverbs 18:9

Change. We can shape the future.

Learning. We need new inputs to keep our minds sharp to create. – Proverbs 15:22

Reflection. Periodic solitude can bring clarity to challenges.

Action. We often find the solution as we try different approaches. – Proverbs 14:23

HOW?

Steps to Implement

Keep your edge. Some entrepreneurs create a business then get bored after the initial excitement. So, what's the key to staying innovative year in and year out? Two things:

1. Love your business – if you love your child, you'll keep investing in helping her develop, right?

2. Embrace the identity of a creator. Do you see yourself and your employees as artists and architects with the ability to make something amazing? The beauty of being an entrepreneur is the freedom to create. It is awesome to think that something of value exists because of me. People gladly part with hard-earned money every day to experience what I created. But if I start to rest on my laurels and run my business three years from now exactly as I do today, that will be a problem.

Pursue many small improvements. Entrepreneurs often risk everything to get their venture off the ground, but once it is stable and profitable, the scale of risk must change. The risks taken to expand products or territories must not be large enough to sink the core business if they go bad. New is not always improved! In 1985, Coke had to bring back its original product after 3 months of poor sales of New Coke. They totally changed the core product that they'd build decades of success around. Disaster!

So, a steady stream of *small* risks is a great recipe to grow a company over time. Some will work, some will not – and you'll learn much from both. Adam Bluestein writes that "placing big bets on high-risk ideas is not only infeasible, it's unwise." In his INC Magazine article, he cites a study revealing that companies find more success in "making incremental changes to improve existing products" and "improving business models, internal processes, and customer experience" ("You're Not That Innovative," September 2013). "Continuous improvement," a key concept in lean manufacturing (see chapter 10), has been embraced as a best practice worldwide. Interestingly, many cultures have sayings for making slow progress over time; in

Haiti, "mache pa mache" ("step by step") denotes the need for patience and perseverance as you move forward slowly. Find satisfaction in making small improvements over and over and over.

Turn challenges into opportunities. As an entrepreneur, you know all too well that problems are not hard to find. They find *you* every day. Use the challenges that present themselves in your business as catalysts for change. You use creativity daily to solve problems. But when the same problem emerges over and over, it's time for a deeper, systemic change. Treat the cause not just the symptom. These are your biggest opportunities to create positive change. But innovation doesn't have to start with a problem. You can take something that's good already – and make it great. Use the questions below to explore potential innovations in your business.

Customer Opportunities:

1. How can we help our potential customers find us more easily?
2. How can we promote our company in ways that reach potential customers?

3. How can we educate potential customers about needs our business can solve?
4. What new initiatives will help build trust with existing customers?
5. How can we provide extraordinary customer care?
6. How can we better please our customers? What do they want?

Product Opportunities:

1. What new products or services would our customers want?
2. How can we improve our current products or services?
3. How can we improve the way we deliver our products or services?
4. How can we improve our processes to decrease waste and increase production?

Employee Opportunities:

1. What can we do to keep our employees engaged and enjoying their jobs?
2. How can we better recognize and reward employee achievement?

3. How can we better collect good ideas from our employees?

4. How can we increase their sense of ownership and responsibility?

Big Picture Opportunities:

1. What are common complaints about our industry? What are ways our company can overcome these barriers, thereby attracting customers and forcing our competitors to improve?

2. How can we learn from competitors and outperform them?

3. Do we need to reinvent our business model?

4. What are the most important challenges facing our company this year?

5. Who are a few businesspeople who'd be willing to help me explore creative solutions to my company's current challenges?

Create a sense of urgency. This is especially necessary for innovations you'll need help from employees to implement. We were a lot more motivated to beef up security after 21 new tires and wheels were stolen right off of our dump trucks in the middle of the night! In his classic book, <u>Leading Change</u>, John Kotter identifies "creating a sense of urgency" as the first step in bringing about effective change in a business. That is common sense, isn't it? Without a strong reason – like a major crisis – people and organizations resist changing the way they do things. Kotter writes in his book: "Never underestimate the magnitude of the forces that reinforce complacency and that help maintain the status quo" (p.42).

Learn. Find out what you *know* you don't know and even what you *don't know* you don't know. Get feedback from clients, employees, trusted friends and family on the issue at hand. Have a discussion with them to stir up group creativity. Some people get more creative a group, and we all need to ask for help when innovating in areas that are outside of our expertise. Friends who see different angles and have complementary skills can significantly enrich what you create. Consult the experts – in person or in print. See how others have solved similar challenges.

Make space to think and write. When are you most creative? Know yourself. What gets your creative juices flowing? For me, I need time alone to think and pray, with a pen and paper. A peaceful outdoor setting helps too.

Give your ideas a quick test run. One of my college art textbooks was titled "Design through Discovery," the idea being that much of the creative process happens along the way as you try out different possibilities. So, without overthinking it, give your new idea a small scale trail launch. (See chapter 9.) The pieces that don't work will spark ideas for improvement. Trial and error is the best way to test out your ideas. Find what works and keep refining it with input from others.

Launch it! Smile. Good work. What's your next challenge? Your "bottleneck" has likely shifted.

Case Study

Here are some ongoing improvements made by two Haitian entrepreneurs despite the crippling fatalism prevalent in their society:

A stone carver named Josue has hired 4 part-time salesmen and has discovered banks and schools to be good new markets for his products. He became president of an association that promotes Haitian culture. He attends their trade shows for free where he finds most of his new customers. He's using his new marketing materials, and has begun putting a label on the back of his plaques with logo and phone number. He's working with the Tourism Department to sell more in Haiti and with the Commerce Department to sell outside of Haiti. He's built a wall for security, built a building for storage, and continues to introduce small product improvements such as different color sand coatings to make the words stand out on his plaques.

A concrete block maker named Nazaire improved his product by producing earthquake resistant blocks, then used his internal cash flow to buy an even better machine that produces more and better blocks. He's recognized that building strong relationships with masons was a key to growing his sales, and now he has 10 masons who buy blocks from him for their projects! Here's an idea that I think is fabulous: he recruited six motorcycle taxi drivers to be part time salesmen, leveraging their mobility and networks of relationships! Always improving.

These innovative entrepreneurs know that if their business isn't moving forward, it's moving backwards. "If you're not growing, you're dying" (Traction p.18). And even though my tree service is 12 years old and is already an industry leader in Orlando, we try to get better all the time. One of our core values is: "improving constantly." Here are the innovations we made in a nine month period: identified 40 potential ways to save money to improve our cash flow and started buying new instead of used heavy equipment to reduce maintenance costs. We got: a better deal on processing credit card payments from customers, a new loan to pay off one with bad terms, and a 550 gallon fuel tank at our second location. We also added a third crew, another salesman, and installed cameras after a theft. Things we improved: uniforms, signs, toll free number, bookkeeping, collections policy and practice, operating agreement, and work schedule. We changed to a different type of corporation, made my brother's ownership share official, and found a better insurance carrier. All in nine months.

Leading Self, Employees, Systems

SELF – Pay attention to what spurs your best ideas. It might be talking to a mentor, reading a book, going to your favorite place, or enjoying your favorite way to relax. It might be a good night's sleep or a discipline that helps you focus. Strangely, just putting a pencil in my hand in front of a blank page signals my brain that it's time to create something new. Whatever it is, space for unhurried reflection is key.

EMPLOYEES – Humans feel most alive when being creative – your employees included! So include them in your drive to innovate. If they're regularly using their brains for creative problem-solving, they'll want to come to work every day.

SYSTEMS – These are among the most powerful innovations you can make. Remember chapter 4: Develop Systems.

NOW WHAT?
Summary

Always making positive changes in your business will keep it fresh for you and be a good model for your employees. If you're not moving forward, you're losing ground to your competitors. Creativity is core to who we are and is bolstered by the belief that we actually *can* affect lasting, positive change. To spur innovation in your business, work to improve in small but steady increments, identify the problems you'd like to solve, learn from clients and employees and experts, make space to think through potential solutions, test out your ideas, and refine them further. Be quick to take action and be tolerant of small failures on the way to big successes. Get better every day.

Application Questions

1. Using the 20 questions in the "steps to implement" section, which areas of your business need your creative attention?
2. What new solutions are your customers asking for?
3. What can you do to create a more conducive environment for your own creativity?
4. How can you encourage and reward innovation in employees?
5. How can you create a culture that embraces change?
6. Are continual small innovations enough to excite you?
7. What game-changing innovations might your company need? How will you manage the associated risks?
8. How would you like your company to impact your industry?
9. Are you more or less innovative than your top competitors?

Recommended Reading

Leading Change by John Kotter

Make it Happen!

What ideas has this chapter stirred in me?

What new light does this chapter shine on my leadership and my business?

What changes do I plan to make?

My actions to *Make it Happen!*	Completion dates	
	Proposed	Actual

Chapter 6 | Overcome Fatalism

By Evan Keller

WHAT?

Definition

With roots in animism, fatalism is a cultural belief that everything that happens is predetermined, so we can't do much to influence our future. Instead of enthusiastically working for positive change today, fatalism causes people to passively wait to see what life will bring to them. It prevents people from making positive changes in their lives and businesses.

Expert Quote

Those in fatalistic cultures tend to be "submissive to events, not goal-oriented nor committed to shaping their own lives and futures….Fatalism makes them hesitant to accept uncertainty, take entrepreneurial risk, and to save" (Daniel Etounga-

Manguelle in <u>Shaping the Developing World</u> by Andy Baker p.169).

Assessment Questions

1. What barriers keep you from making improvements you know you should make in your business?
2. Do you delay these new initiative as you wait for your circumstances to improve?
3. Do you believe that you can influence your future?
4. What are your views of good and evil in this present world?
5. How do you see your own identity and role in this world?

WHY?

Benefits

Innovation. When removing the major barrier of fatalistic thinking, it's easier to pursue the creative improvements described in the previous chapter.

Positivity. Evil – while very present in our world – is limited by an omnipotent God who only allows what will shape us for good. While we suffer in this life, Christ bears our pain with us and we will share in his ultimate victory and glory.

Achievement. When replacing the shackles of fatalism with a biblical vision of co-laboring with the Almighty, we can accomplish great things.

Barriers

Invisibility. Cultural beliefs are even harder to change when you don't consciously articulate them.

Entrenched thinking. Deeply rooted thinking is hard to uproot.

Survival mentality. Building a thriving tomorrow is vastly different than merely living for today.

Lack of trust. Depending on a good God and interdepending on other seems foreign in a culture of mistrust.

Underlying Values

Initiative. God delights in our efforts, and blesses our initiatives for good. – Hebrews 11:32-34

Work ethic. Knowing our God-given work matters, we put our hearts into it. – Colossians 3:23

Identity. As children of the King, we are destined to rule. We can begin to lead boldly in this life – for his glory. – Romans 8:14-19

Courage. We face the future and enemies both visible and invisible knowing that God's purposes for us and through us will prevail. – Joshua 1:9-11

HOW?

Steps to Implement

Realize the power of cultural beliefs. Our cultural beliefs have a strong influence on how we live. Our society's perceptions about life are so ingrained in us that we often don't even notice their presence and influence on us. Does a fish know it's in water? We hardly think about the air we breathe until it's missing. Even though we take them for granted, we're extremely dependent on things like air and sunlight. We may not think much about our cultural beliefs, yet they quietly and profoundly shape our thoughts and attitudes, decisions and actions. There is good and bad in every culture. Some cultural beliefs reflect God's truth, while others are distortions of it. For example, United States culture tells me I can achieve anything I set my mind to, but it also pushes me to achieve even if it causes me to ignore my family and become addicted to work, money and power. Many Americans don't realize they need to be in control, are bossy, and think everything should be done their way, and done *right now!* Even in this very book I want to influence the way you think and operate your businesses even though my understanding of how things work in your country is very limited. It's very hard for any of us to operate outside of our cultural beliefs!

Recognize fatalistic thinking. Here's what fatalism looks like in entrepreneurs: They're stuck in the past, and haven't continued to make positive changes on a regular basis. They still do things just like they did years ago, and don't pursue goals. They don't sacrifice their time and money to build for the future. They won't invest in their employees because they are suspicious they'll become competitors. Thus with only a sole leader, their businesses cannot grow into strong companies. Like most of the people around them, they are just trying to survive today. They are reactive rather than proactive – seeing themselves as being *acted upon* by others, whether by competitors, corrupt government officials, economic conditions, or spirits/ancestors/fate. These forces have frozen them in fear. This limits their sense of responsibility, and also severely limits their potential. They're passive and resigned, afraid to try anything new until market circumstances improve. They see competitors capturing part of their market share, but they won't risk making a change that might attract more customers. Everything is on hold. They're waiting for something: a loan to come in, the election to be over, a competitor to drop out, or the economy to improve.

Renew your mind. Like I said, it's very hard to act against the beliefs of our culture – but it's not impossible! It requires building new patterns of belief and thought, which takes time and spiritual transformation. So meditate on the truths of Scripture, act on them, and pray that God's Spirit will plant them deeply in you while rooting out the lies of fatalism. Do these things consistently over time to renew your mind. "You shall know the truth, and the truth shall set you free" (John 8:32).

Meditate on these biblical truths:

1. Time is consecutive, not cyclical, providing opportunities for real progress.
2. We are children of God who are destined to share in his glory.
3. His glory begins to shine through us as we carry out his work in this world.
4. God is with us so we can live with courage rather than fear.
5. Even though evil still clouds our world, its defeat is certain for its power will be easily destroyed by our omnipotent God who is in ultimate control.
6. Even when evil forces oppose us, God is with us and his purposes for us will prevail.
7. When we struggle to do something good, the Lord supports us with his strength.

8. God wants to work through us to bless our communities.

Meditate on these Scriptures, looking for the seven truths listed above:

2 Thessalonians 1:11-12

¹¹ With this in mind, we constantly pray for you, that our God may make you worthy of his calling, and that by his power he may bring to fruition your every desire for goodness and your every deed prompted by faith. ¹² We pray this so that the name of our Lord Jesus may be glorified in you, and you in him, according to the grace of our God and the Lord Jesus Christ.

Romans 8:14-19

¹⁴ For those who are led by the Spirit of God are the children of God. ¹⁵ The Spirit you received does not make you slaves, so that you live in fear again; rather, the Spirit you received brought about your adoption to sonship. And by him we cry, *"Abba, Father."* ¹⁶ The Spirit himself testifies with our spirit that we are God's children. ¹⁷ Now if we are children, then we are heirs— heirs of God and co-heirs with Christ, if indeed we share in his sufferings in order that we may also share in his glory.

[18] I consider that our present sufferings are not worth comparing with the glory that will be revealed in us. [19] For the creation waits in eager expectation for the children of God to be revealed.

2 Kings 6:13-18

[13] "Go, find out where he is," the king ordered, "so I can send men and capture him." The report came back: "He is in Dothan." [14] Then he sent horses and chariots and a strong force there. They went by night and surrounded the city.

[15] When the servant of the man of God got up and went out early the next morning, an army with horses and chariots had surrounded the city. "Oh no, my lord! What shall we do?" the servant asked.

[16] "Don't be afraid," the prophet answered. "Those who are with us are more than those who are with them."

[17] And Elisha prayed, "Open his eyes, Lord, so that he may see." Then the Lord opened the servant's eyes, and he looked and saw the hills full of horses and chariots of fire all around Elisha.

¹⁸ As the enemy came down toward him, Elisha prayed to the Lord, "Strike this army with blindness." So he struck them with blindness, as Elisha had asked.

Hebrews 11:32-34

³² And what more shall I say? I do not have time to tell about Gideon, Barak, Samson and Jephthah, about David and Samuel and the prophets, ³³ who through faith conquered kingdoms, administered justice, and gained what was promised; who shut the mouths of lions, ³⁴ quenched the fury of the flames, and escaped the edge of the sword; whose weakness was turned to strength; and who became powerful in battle and routed foreign armies.

1 John 4:3-4

³ but every spirit that does not acknowledge Jesus is not from God. This is the spirit of the antichrist, which you have heard is coming and even now is already in the world.

⁴ You, dear children, are from God and have overcome them, because the one who is in you is greater than the one who is in the world.

Joshua 1:9-11

⁹ Have I not commanded you? Be strong and courageous. Do not be afraid; do not be discouraged, for the Lord your God will be with you wherever you go."

¹⁰ So Joshua ordered the officers of the people: ¹¹ "Go through the camp and tell the people, 'Get your provisions ready. Three days from now you will cross the Jordan here to go in and take possession of the land the Lord your God is giving you for your own.'"

Ephesians 2:10

¹⁰ For we are God's handiwork, created in Christ Jesus to do good works, which God prepared in advance for us to do.

Develop a supportive community. Find other entrepreneurs who also want to be transformed by God through Scripture, prayer, and mutual encouragement. Meet regularly to help each other grow. Help each other live out this biblical vision of working alongside the Creator to create ways to better serve your community.

Case Study

Fatalism is deeply engrained in Haitian culture, yet there are companies which have broken free from its immobilizing grip. A communications company based in nearby Jamaica, Digicel is the most recognizable company in Haiti. It is known for constantly inventing new solutions for its customers. It openly defies fatalistic thinking: "Our belief is that anything and everything is possible....Digicel is always seeking the next challenge, breaking barriers to provide solutions to what others thought not possible." Likewise, a smaller company called Enersa is Haiti's only manufacturer of solar panels, known best for its innovative (theft-proof and hurricane proof) solar street lights, which it has installed in over 70 Haitian cities with underdeveloped electric infrastructure. With coaching from Partners Worldwide, they are excelling in their market where both jobs and street lights are rare.

Leading Self, Employees, Systems

SELF – Identify any descriptions that apply to you in the "recognize fatalistic thinking" section and outline your strategy to renew your mind.

EMPLOYEES – Lead by example to nurture a culture of trust, positivity, hard work, initiative, and sacrifice for the future.

SYSTEMS – Practice spiritual disciplines of prayer and meditation on Scripture. Pursue positive change in your business through goal-setting (chapter 3) and constant innovation (chapter 5).

NOW WHAT?

Summary

If you believe and act on these truths, they will change your life, your family, and your business. I encourage you to spend time immersing yourselves in the Scriptures which teach these truths, and diligently pray for God to replace fatalism's lies with these truths, so that they become stronger forces in your lives than any cultural belief. Rather than waiting and wishing for something good to happen to them, you are empowered by God to make change happen in your business and for your community.

Application Questions

1. What in these Scriptures is hardest for you to believe and act on?

2. What is the difference between how you see yourself and how these Scriptures define your identity?

3. How should these Scriptures influence how you run your business?

4. How will you apply the discipline of prayer to these issues?

5. Who can you gather for regular support, prayer and accountability?

Recommended Reading

The Central Liberal Truth by Laurence E. Harrison

Make it Happen!

What ideas has this chapter stirred in me?

What new light does this chapter shine on my leadership and my business?

What changes do I plan to make?

My actions to *Make it Happen!*	Completion dates	
	Proposed	Actual

GrowBook Action Plan
by Evan Keller, June 2017

Circle the appropriate action for each topic:

1. **Lead Yourself** - *Am I intentionally investing in my personal relationships, growth, and health?*

    Maintain   Fine-Tune   Overhaul

2. **Set the Course** - *Have I written my company vision, mission, and values? Do I ensure that everything else aligns with them?*

    Maintain   Fine-Tune   Overhaul

3. **Pursue Goals** - *Have I written goals for this year and do I faithfully pursue them?*

    Maintain   Fine-Tune   Overhaul

4. **Develop Systems** - *Do I write, implement, and improve employee processes to increase efficiency in my operations and consistency to my customers?*

    Maintain   Fine-Tune   Overhaul

5. **Innovate Constantly** - *Am I always finding ways to improve my business?*

    Maintain   Fine-Tune   Overhaul

6. **Overcome Fatalism** - *Do you believe the truth that you are empowered to positively shape your future?*

    Maintain   Fine-Tune   Overhaul

MY #1 FOCUS: _____

Center your marketing messages on customer needs. Until you have more customers than you can serve, make it your number one priority to find them online and face-to-face.

Chapter 7 | Craft Customer-Focused Branding

By Evan Keller

WHAT?

Definition

"Brand" is a broad term for your company's perceived identity, personality, and unique customer solutions. Although your brand refers to your company image as a whole, it should be most clearly and succinctly communicated through your name, tagline, and logo along with its associated colors, fonts and images. These tools should connect effectively with your target market, hinting at attractive solutions that you offer to them. Your broader message should flow from these highly concentrated communications.

Expert Quote

"Proverbs are the Holy Grail of simplicity. Coming up with a short, compact phrase is easy. Anybody can do it. On the other hand, coming up with a profound compact phrase is incredibly difficult." – Chip & Dan Heath <u>Made To Stick</u> p.62

Assessment Questions

1. Why did you (or someone else) give your business the name it has? How well does it align with your vision and target market?

2. Does your name immediately communicate what you do? Is it customer-focused, hinting at the solutions you bring?

3. What is your logo and tag line? How well do they represent your business and connect with customers?

WHY?

Benefits

Attraction. Good branding creates an immediate "yes" in your ideal customer's mind. It evokes a positive feeling that is a great first step in building trust – the foundation of business.

Condensed communication. Good branding says a lot with very little. It's a highly concentrated dose of you. It quickly relays a large amount of information that would take a long time to consciously articulate. Like it or not, it sums you up. So make sure it says what you want it to say.

Loyalty. If you deliver on what your brand promises, your branding will reinforce customer loyalty.

Barriers

Bad Design. It's everywhere and it's fuelled by unqualified designers and cheap customers.

Cost. Good design isn't cheap – but is worth every penny. Remember, it's a long-term investment that works for you every single day. If you don't pay enough to a proven designer, you may not get their best work.

Clutter. Entrepreneurs try to say too much with their logos and end up saying nothing because they fail to capture and keep attention. "If you say three things, you don't say anything." – Chip & Dan Heath <u>Made to Stick</u> p.33

Delegation. It's amazing how quickly and easily entrepreneurs give a designer they even don't know control over their company identity. No matter how much help you get, you should choose not only your name but your tagline. Don't design your own logo, but know exactly what you want it to communicate, and stay involved in every step of the process. Make sure the final product is amazing and represents your company perfectly.

Underlying Values

Clarity. In a world jammed with visual clutter, a good brand simplifies your message for quick consumption. Visual clarity of your brand is contingent on your clear vision for your company.

If you don't know who you are, where you're going, and what you do best, you have no chance of communicating it clearly.

Centering on customers. Instead of only talking about yourself, your brand should be focused on the customer needs you meet. – Philippians 2:4

Respect for words. For something as central to the identity of a business, some don't value branding enough to give it their full attention. Words and images have incredible power to move the mind, will, and emotions. – Proverbs 18:21

Consistency. Customers want a predictably good experience from you. Consistent use of your brand says that you are a reliable provider of what they need.

HOW?

Steps to Implement

Reflect on what makes you unique. Branding is a way of defining your business. What are your core products and services, and what is distinct about how you deliver them? This is your "value proposition" – why people buy from you. "Branding is about the promise of a distinct, memorable experience. It's about creating an expectation and delivering it consistently" (Giuli Schacht of Rational Developments, Inc.)

Know your target market and how you uniquely meet their needs. Make sure your branding does a great job of connecting what you do best to those who value it most. See more on identifying your target market in chapter 7 and meeting their needs in chapter 9.

Choose a company name that is short, memorable, and at least hints at what you can do for customers. Your company name should embody your value proposition and your core products. "Tree Work Now" says exactly what my customers need after a Florida thunderstorm. "Creating Jobs" names the most important and desirable outcome of our non-profit organization.

Avoid these naming pitfalls. Unless you have millions to make your brand a household name, don't name it after yourself – make it about your clients, not you. In a seminar at the national university of Honduras, Jeff Hostetter (a lead mentor with Creating Jobs Inc) advised business students against naming their businesses after themselves, adding this question: "Who would want to buy a business named after you?" A recent INC Magazine study shows that naming your business after yourself can stunt its growth (Bobbie Gossage, "Made for Speed" May 2015, p.92). And by all means, don't put an acronym in your name, which is a colossal waste of your most valuable communication opportunity. Despite this obvious fact, business owners often include acronyms or words that are unrecognizable to their target audience. Unbelievable. Also, beware of nearsighted branding that forces you into too narrow of a geographic scope or line of products. For example, I began my business with my county name in my business name, not realizing we'd quickly grow beyond our county. Remembering my mistake, I discouraged a friend from putting one of his many services in his business name. He's happy he replaced "lawn" with "property maintenance," which has enabled his strong growth in pressure washing, pool cleaning, and handyman services.

Grow as a writer. This is one of life's most important skills. And unless you plan to run your business alone, communication will be key to inspire, motivate, encourage, and train your employees. Read and apply books like Roy Peter Clark's <u>Writing Tools</u>.

Write your own tagline and incorporate it into your logo. Incorporate some of Chip & Dan Heath's six principles of sticky ideas: simple, unexpected, concrete, credible, emotional, and stories (<u>Made to Stick</u>).

Give your tagline double duty. Target your tagline primarily to customers, but make it powerful enough to be meaningful within your company as well. Your branding is more authentic when it speaks to how things actually are with your employees as well as how outsiders see you. You have integrity if your message matches "who you are when no one's looking." Here's how branding is used internally in my two ventures. I coined "Every Detail. Every Time." to be our motto as well as tagline at Tree Work Now Inc. I use it as a mantra I want in my employees' minds as they make countless small decisions throughout the course of their workdays. Using only three unique words, the repetition powerfully communicates a commitment that will not be deterred. It is the answer to every question of whether or not they should do a little extra to make things a little better. This is essential to our goal of raising the industry standard. With Creating Jobs Inc, "Business for Global Good" is our vision as well as our tagline. By combining only four quite common words, it paints the lofty hoped-for result of our organization's existence. Your tagline might not be your vision statement as well, but should flow from your overall vision and strategy.

Include your Website address. If your web address is the same as your business name and your website is a primary way customers find you, include your domain extension in your logo. My two ventures have "TreeWorkNow.com" and "CreatingJobs.org" in their logos. This invites those who encounter us for the first time to explore and connect with us further. Years of our truck signs crisscrossing Central Florida has brought is many customers and helped us capture dominant market share.

Choose your font. I chose the exact fonts for both my logos by looking at various font libraries online. These sites allow you to plug in your name to see what it will look like in various fonts before you buy (for an average of $45). Find the category of fonts that best embodies your company, and then narrow it down to your top ten. Print out your name in those ten styles, then ponder it for a few days and get input from people with good design sense. Narrow it to 1-3 fonts. Give these to your designer, but be open to his/her suggestions as well. Even if one of yours isn't the final choice, you communicated much about who you are to a designer who likely didn't know anything about you or your business.

Choose imagery, if any. Your logo can be great with typography only, but can be enhanced with graphics as long as your name remains prominent. I didn't technically design the leaf (also used in this book) in my Tree Work Now logo, but I gave detailed conceptual instructions and critiqued each draft until I got exactly what was in my mind's eye. Know what you want. Get what you want. Make sure the imagery looks good when small enough to fit on a business card. Look at the major brands you use daily – most are iconic, simple, elegant, looking equally good tiny or huge.

Choose your colors. In most cases, one or two colors are best to retain simplicity, power, and clarity. This also makes it more cost effective to print in certain formats. Learn about color theory to make sure you communicate what you intend. Don't automatically default to colors that are standard in your industry. Being "unexpected" is one of <u>Made to Stick</u>'s six principles of sticky ideas.

Choose a shape. Think about the most important places your logo will be displayed. Make sure your logo will look good in those spots. Bring a suggested height-to-width ratio to your designer. If necessary, have a horizontal and vertical version to fit in different contexts, but make one primary. This allows you to make sure your logo is never stretched out of its original proportions. In design speak: maintain the original "aspect ratio" whenever enlarging or reducing the logo's size. Squished or stretched lettering looks horrid. If you're sloppy with your own identity, why should customers believe you'll provide good value for their money?

Choose a designer to implement your vision. Find a graphic designer from trusted referrals or better yet, chose a designer of a logo you love which masterfully embodies the company it represents. In any case, never hire a designer without seeing lots of their work and being confident that their style is fitting and talent level is superb. If one designer isn't the obvious choice and within your budget, interview two or three and get their initial impressions of the direction they'd take with the preparation you've already done. Designers like clients who know what they want.

Get original art files. When the design is complete, make sure the artist gives you the original art files – usually an Adobe Illustrator file (.ai or .eps) – so that you can get higher resolution images and have it on hand for any changes you decide to make in the future. Also request both high and low resolution versions (.jpg or .gif) in both color and black/white (for single-color applications). Make sure you are the unrestricted owner (not licensee) of the artwork.

Rebrand if necessary. If your existing brand doesn't make a splendid connection to your target market, consider a name change and/or a logo change. This is a major decision that shouldn't be taken lightly. It will cost you a lot in the short-term – potential loss of customers, and the time/money to change it on all your official documents and marketing communications. But, you must make this decision with a long-term view. Will this make a major positive impact on my company in 3, 5, and 10 years? If the answer is yes, then it must be done. Don't delay.

The longer you wait, the longer it will take you to re-establish brand awareness and grow your market share.

Broadcast your brand. Put your brand identity everywhere you can and ensure all company communications are consistent with your name, tagline, color scheme, and graphics style. Your brand is the headline – all other communications follow from it. These guidelines will get you started in building a brand that people trust and are loyal to.

Create consistent communications that flow from your brand and center on your customers' needs. In a shoddy industry, our branding exudes professionalism – from the intricate leaf graphic to the website represented by the ".com" in our logo. Here's how we expounded on our tagline ("Every Detail. Every Time.") in our advertising….I did some analysis of what our customers want by tallying up 297 responses to the question: "What factors are most important to you when hiring a tree service?" I compiled and studied the results and made the following headline and ad copy to tell customers we were focused on their needs:

We Know What You Want. We Deliver It.

From asking hundreds of our customers what they deem important, we know that fair and affordable pricing matters to you most. You also value highly skilled crews who will safeguard your property and clean up thoroughly. You want a company you can depend on to show up and perform the work as promised. Fulfilling these requirements is our highest priority.

Case Study

Saul Contrares' company is called Ser Movil, which sounds like a mobile phone company to the average Honduran. Aside from pest control, he has a second completely different line of business – the installation and cleaning of water cisterns. We helped him market those separate divisions under separate brands, to marvelous affect. Separate logos advance his two brands: ProLimpio and XPlagas. This helped Saul produce strong results within a year, including a 59% increase in sales, 3 new jobs, and 98% client satisfaction.

Leading Self, Employees, Systems

SELF – You are the keeper of the brand. Watch over its careful development and consistent use. Don't content yourself with delegating this; it's too important.

EMPLOYEES – Make sure it is used in all company communication – internal as well as external – since branding can help build loyalty among employees as well as customers – if you actually live out what the brand communicates.

SYSTEMS – Carefully crafting and consistently using your branding are important processes.

NOW WHAT?

Summary

Since branding is so central to your company's identity and is often the first point of contact with potential customers, you should direct its development. Choose a company name and tagline that speak to your customers' needs, and give detailed input to the proven graphic designer who is producing your logo. Rebranding has a high cost, but if your branding doesn't resonate with customers and reveal your unique solutions, the long-term benefits of rebranding are worth the short-term growing pains. All of your company communications should be reflections of your clear, strong branding.

Application Questions

1. Have you clearly articulated what you do best and how you uniquely meet customer needs?
2. Are you up for the hands-on involvement I'm advising?
3. Which professional and amateur writers and editors you can consult?
4. How will you find the right graphic designer?
5. Are you willing to pay enough to get good design?
6. Do you need to rebrand?
7. What inconsistencies in the display of your logo need to be corrected?
8. What company communications do you need to realign to your branding?

Recommended Reading

<u>Made to Stick</u> by Chip & Dan Heath

Make it Happen!

What ideas has this chapter stirred in me?

What new light does this chapter shine on my leadership and my business?

What changes do I plan to make?

My actions to *Make it Happen!*	Completion dates	
	Proposed	Actual

Chapter 8 | Generate a Sufficient Flow of Customers

By Evan Keller

WHAT?

Definition

A strong flow of clients is your biggest business need. You can have the world's best product, but if people don't know about it, you have no business. Lead generation is about finding potential customers and demonstrating value that moves them to action. Until your business has a sufficient flow of customers, you must identify and pursue your target market with organized, undaunted, top-priority effort.

Expert Quote

Lead generation involves "identifying people with needs you can satisfy and telling them so in ways they can understand quickly and easily." - Michael Gerber in <u>E-Myth Mastery</u>).

Assessment Questions

1. Is your revenue where it should be given the age of your business? Are you experiencing healthy revenue growth?

2. Are you producing at 75% or more capacity (with current facilities, equipment, and employees)?

3. If you have capacity to serve more customers, how much time do you spend finding them?

4. Do you know who your ideal customers are and are you reaching them?

5. Do you have enough market share to be known as a leader in your industry?

6. Would your business still be profitable if you lost your top three customers?

WHY?

Benefits

Sales. More sales follow more leads – without a steady stream of customers, you have a hobby, not a business.

Profitable relationships. Success in business rests on finding, landing, and satisfying customers –day after day, year after year.

Market research. Interacting regularly with potential customers keeps you in tune with what they want.

Barriers

Inertia. It's hard to change your work patterns to spend more time reaching potential customers.

Risk aversion. It's easier to stick with what you know, doing whatever business task you feel competent in. If you don't have enough customers, then it's time to build a new competency. Become an expert on finding customers who value your products and services enough to part with cash. Customers aren't as scary as you think, and hearing "no" is just a step toward hearing "yes".

Important distractions. Technicians can be hired or developed, but no one will build your business but you. The best entrepreneurs focus on crafting innovative products and relentlessly finding customers who need them. Hire others to do the rest. Some business owners get so busy a technician that they fool themselves into thinking it is the main thing, that being product experts will somehow make their business boom. "If you want to work *in* a business, get a job in somebody else's business! But don't go to work in your own. Because while you're working…there's important work you're *not* doing, the strategic work, the entrepreneurial work that will lead your business forward" (Michael Gerber, <u>E-Myth Revisited</u> p.39). Until you've built an awesome lead generation system that brings in more potential customers than you can serve, your most strategic job is chief marketing officer.

Underlying Values

Determination. Find every possible good source of leads. – Proverbs 24:16

Initiative. Get out and chase customers. – Ecclesiastes 11:4

Positivity. Be undaunted by the word "no."

Focus. Know who wants and can afford your product. Focus on them.

Trust. Entrust employees with duty you need to take off to enable your focus. – 2 Timothy 2:2

Discipline. Do the hard thing that brings growth – over and over and over. – 2 Timothy 2:3-6

Wisdom. Discern what your business needs most from you at this stage of its life.

HOW?

Steps to Implement

<u>Identify Your Target Market.</u> Who and where are your best potential customers? Who wants and can afford what you sell? There are two elements to your target market:

1. **Demographic Scope.** Which of the following traits are relevant to identifying your best customers? <u>For people</u>: age, gender, occupation, income, employment status, education, marital status, family status, race, language, interests, affiliations, and home ownership. <u>For organizations</u>: industry, product lines, size of business,

type of business, geographic coverage, and financial status (Michael Gerber <u>E-Myth Mastery</u> p.127). Some entrepreneurs try to sell to everyone, but end up with no one. "An army everywhere is an army nowhere" (Sun Tzu <u>The Art of War</u>). Although I see many insurance messages and agencies, the one that really caught my attention was a simple, tiny sign that said "Insurance for Diabetics." Even though I'm not diabetic and not shopping for insurance, that message has stuck with me because they seem to have found an exceptional solution for a specific segment of the population.

2. **Geographic Scope.** Just as it is difficult to maintain close relationships over long distances, cost-effective delivery usually has limits. Who *can't* you afford to sell to? Is your current geographic scope large enough to sustain long-term growth? If both your *demographic* and *geographic* scopes are very narrow, then you need a wider range of products and services to keep growing your company over time.

<u>**Engage your target market.**</u> Now that you know who and where your potential customers are, how will you connect them to your company? What lead generation channels will best reach them?

1. **Leverage existing relationships.** Since business is built on trust, you'll want to reach out to people you already know to directly do business with you and to connect you with their networks of people who need what you sell. Assuming you've built up some relational equity, friends and acquaintances will be glad to help you. You can cross-sell and set up recurring sales programs for existing customers. Some of your lapsed customers may be ready to place another order. The customers you've recently satisfied are eager to give you referrals, so ask them while their good experience is still fresh and offer them a small thank you gift (we give out tons of $25 restaurant gift cards) or small discount on their next purchase.

2. **Go in person.** Identify 50-100 major potential customers and go to see them in person. Don't delegate. Don't email. Don't procrastinate. Just go! Develop face-to-face relationships with folks who can make a big difference in growing your business. Because trust is best built face-to-face, this approach is far better than phoning or emailing. Plus getting attention from a stranger is pretty hard if not face-to-face. You have a better chance of reaching them and you can put your marketing materials right in their hands. You can read body language and make a personal connection. My first

– and short-lived – salesman became an expert at making gorgeous and detailed data bases of major potential customers to go see – but he never went! Don't get stuck in the research stage - break inertia, create momentum. Admit that you feel safer in the office. Don't waste hours and days making the perfect plan, which for some is a way of delaying the hard but effective part. Don't get stuck in the paralysis of analysis. Face your fear head-on with positive action. Knowing what to do and actually doing it are quite different! Remember the thrill of selling – that will reinforce you once you get started. Make it a priority by reserve huge chunks in your schedule, perhaps two whole days or three half days a week to go out and sell. For what to do when you arrive, see chapter 11 on sales.

3. **Try everything.** In the early years of marketing Tree Work Now Inc, I focused my creative energy on drawing in a steady stream of customers in every way I could imagine. We did it all – even had our tree climbers hanging off the sides of our dump trucks in a Christmas parade (and won first place). I tried everything; including guerrilla marketing! We advertised everywhere - from billboards to phone books to community newsletters to sport stadiums. I installed large truck signs with our website address and a memorable toll free

number (855-WE-PRUNE). I networked at Rotary Club and the chamber of commerce. I networked with landscapers and lawn maintenance companies and got lots of jobs by offering referral fees to them. I tried all kinds of advertising and spent lots of time and money building the best Google-optimized website in the industry, along with strategies to get noticed online.

4. **Harness the power of trust.** Establish a presence on trust-building marketing channels, such as websites that have online reviews, Chambers of Commerce, and industry associations – especially those which grant accreditations your customers trust.

5. **Harness the power of tribalism.** Whereas most advertising doesn't catch the attention of its target market, people slow down and pay attention when at "home" in their own "tribe." For example, people care about their own neighborhoods, clubs, places of worship, schools, hobbies, activities, sports, and favorite charities. If you can make meaningful alliances with these associations that have captured the heart of your target market, there's a better chance they'll hear and respond to your message. So sponsoring your daughter's soccer team might bring more leads to your construction company than an ad in the phone book. Advertising in a neighborhood association newsletter in a

neighborhood to which you'd like to expand your housecleaning services would be better than advertising in the city newspaper. Or get a nonprofit you and your target market cares about to promote your business as its top donor. When a bank agreed to sponsor our Paddle Out Poverty paddleboard race that benefits Creating Jobs Inc, I naturally got my next four equipment loans from them. They touched my heart and I wanted to say thanks. That's the magic of tribalism.

6. **Improve Google rankings.** Since many purchases (in some countries) start with a local internet search, I recommend you take these simple but powerful steps toward achieving top Google rankings: add regular content, embed the right keywords, build many consistent citations, optimize your Google+ page, and request Google reviews. According to Moz.com, these are some of the easiest, highest impact actions you can take boost your rankings. See more at: https://moz.com/local-search-ranking-factors. Here's how to take the five steps:

   A. **Add regular, valuable content.** Be sure to write unique and useful information for your site so that over time it becomes an authoritative source in your industry. "Content" is mostly well-written, relevant text, but also includes good photos and especially videos. Here are brief content tips directly from Google: https://support.google.com/webmasters/answer/6001093?hl=en

B. **Embed the right keywords.** "Keywords" are words or phrases that you think customers will type in a search to find the products or services you offer. You should choose your most important keywords and then intentionally embed them into your website, including in your code, content, and web address. This article addresses all facets of using keywords: http://backlinko.com/keyword-research. And here are several keyword tools to help you identify your own: http://www.pamorama.net/2014/01/04/10-keyword-research-tools/

C. **Build many consistent citations.** Completely fill out free profiles on directories such as internet yellow pages and any directories used in your industry. Uploading your basic business info on such sites is considered a "citation." The most important thing I can say about your citations is that the info on each one should be absolutely identical. So standardize your name, address, phone and website address, so all are listed the same across the internet.

D. **Optimize your Google My Business page.** Go to Google My Business and claim your business if you haven't already. Build out your complete profile with physical address, hours of operation, photos and videos, tagline and introduction. Link it to your website. Be sure to get this one right because the experts say this is the single most important factor in Google rankings. Here is how to optimize your page: http://blog.hubspot.com/marketing/how-to-siphon-seo-value-from-google-plus-slideshare

E. **Request Google reviews.** Google values the quantity, velocity, and diversity of your reviews. Because leaving a review requires customers to have a Google+ account, many who promise to write a review never do. Others are too busy or just forget, so you'll have to ask a lot of people to get a few reviews. We ask every happy customer. Here are best practices for gathering reviews: http://www.localvisibilitysystem.com/2013/04/04/the-complete-guide-to-google-pluslocal-reviews-and-especially-how-to-get-them/.

F. **Refine your strategy by tracking lead sources and conversion rates.** Ask every customer: "How did you find us?" See what works and do more of that. Record how many leads – and actual sales – come from each lead generation channel. The conversion rates and selling prices will tell you about the quality of leads coming from different sources. After trying everything for a while, this analysis will help refine your strategy – funnelling your time and money into the most effective channels. My marketing budget was once 10% of revenue, but is now 1% since I've found out what works for us, and because our inexpensive online lead generation is so strong.

7. **Delegate operations so you can focus on lead generation.** It's a good idea to delegate some of the operational aspects of your business to capable employees, providing additional training as necessary. (See more in chapter 13.) For example, as soon as I could find people whose expertise exceeded my own, I delegated tasks so I could focus on growing the business. Most tree business owners become experts at the technical skills of using ropes and heavy equipment, but never learn how to grow a business. I did the opposite and we quickly captured significant market share all across Central Florida. In those beginning years, I made generating leads the biggest priority – even ahead of developing a great product! I gave it as much time as it needed, and I poured my creative energy and strategic thinking into it. I knew that without a strong and

growing customer base, my business would never thrive. In the first few months of starting my business, I knocked on doors every afternoon and all day Saturday introducing myself to homeowners. I needed to generate revenue even before I had good marketing materials or equipment; I had no capital or even good tree trimming skills – I just sold my smile, then added equipment and talented employees and advertising from the sales I generated by knocking on doors. Do you see yourself as a product-maker or business-builder? Are you a technician or an entrepreneur?

Case Study

A friend with a brick paver business bought a large property where he spent months building an elaborate showroom for his work. He built a fire pit, outdoor kitchen, fountains, and various paver patterns meticulously laid out. He put a lot of money and time and love into it…but few customers ever saw it, leaving him with little business and lots of debt. He thought: "If I build it, they will come!" He was wrong and his business died. Another friend runs a car garage which hasn't changed its look or customer service approach in 25 years. I asked how he attracts new clients. "I don't have time for that. I can hardly keep up with all the changes in automobile technology these days." He needs to work on his business and hire mechanics to work on the cars. Until he makes that shift, he'll have a job – not a company. A good technician is often a horrible entrepreneur. On the positive side, Saul Contrares took our advice to appoint 12-year employee Margarita to oversee operations of his Honduran pest control company. This freed him up to generate new leads, which is part of why his revenue increased 59% in a single year.

Leading Self, Employees, Systems

SELF – Do what you know you need to do. What I'm writing is plain common sense. People intuitively know this, but they don't do it. Strong entrepreneurs lead the charge in building their businesses. They get it done.

EMPLOYEES – As already noted, employees can step up oversight of operations to free up the entrepreneur to find new customers. While the business owner should lead the way, employees can work on lead generation in various ways, including implementing the following systems.

SYSTEMS – Increase sales opportunities with: recurring sales program, cross-selling process, referral program, scheduling regular blocks of time, and maintaining a database of current leads to pursue.

NOW WHAT?

Summary

Until your business is generating more high quality leads than you can handle, you should invest the lion-share of your time and creative energy to attracting and satisfying new customers. It requires delegating production tasks to free up your time, shifting your mindset from technician to strategist, and overcoming inertia. This prepares you to identify and engage your target market with creative energy, leveraging existing relationships, going in person and online. Try various ways of attracting your target market, track the results, and refine your approach.

Application Questions

1. What operational duties do you need to free yourself from in order to chase new customers?
2. What is the demographic and geographic scope of your target market?
3. What new ways of engaging your target market will you try?
4. Are potential customers searching on the internet for what you sell?
5. How will you better track the quantity and quality of leads from various sources?
6. What fears hold you back from engaging potential customers? How will you overcome them?
7. How much time do you need to devote to lead generation – especially to visiting major potential customers in person?
8. What activities will you *stop* doing to free up time for this?
9. Who are the biggest potential customers that you want to land? How will you go about it?

Recommended Reading

E-Myth Mastery by Michael E. Gerber

Make it Happen!

What ideas has this chapter stirred in me?

What new light does this chapter shine on my leadership and my business?

What changes do I plan to make?

My actions to *Make it Happen!*	Completion dates	
	Proposed	Actual

Circle the appropriate action for each topic:

7. **Craft Customer-Focused Branding** - *Have I developed a name, tagline, and logo that speaks to my customers' needs and reveals my unique solutions?*

                Maintain   Fine-Tune   Overhaul

8. **Generate a Sufficient Flow of Customers** - *Do I have a strong lead generation system? If not, am I spending considerable time pursuing potential customers?*

                Maintain   Fine-Tune   Overhaul

MY #1 FOCUS: _____

3. Production

Provide solutions that customers crave and use customer feedback to improve them. Work to produce with ever-increasing efficiency.

Chapter 9 | Create Unique Customer Solutions

By Evan Keller

WHAT?

Definition

Your core products and services should bring marry your top skills with the market needs you can meet better than anyone else. New products should align with your foundational documents as well as your branding, and not divert that company focus or derail your cash flow. Market tests them before final development and release.

Expert Quote

"A company gets better at the things it practices. Practice quality, and you get better at quality. But quality takes time, so by working solely on quality, you end up losing something else that's important – speed....In many ways, we're returning to our roots: quick, scrappy, and impatient up front; quality obsessed, careful, and thoughtful later on" (Jason Fried, CEO of 37 Signals, Inc Magazine, May 2013, p.37).

Assessment Questions

1. Are you experiencing steady revenue growth with your existing products?

2. Are your products and services in higher demand than your competitors'?

3. What are your customers asking for that would fit well with your company identity and focus?

4. What new products would marry your top skills with market needs that you can meet better than anyone else?

5. Are new products your best growth strategy or would it be wiser to sell your existing products in new markets?

WHY?

Benefits

Security. Offering something people consistently want gives you a place in the market. Providing superior solutions will help you keep that niche.

Growth. New products are promising avenues for growth, especially if you can cross-sell them to your existing network of customers. Diversification can reduce risk.

Edge. Launching new products is one way to keep your creativity sharp and your team energized.

Barriers

Funding. New products can require lots of capital for research, development, raw materials, machinery, personnel, and marketing.

Fatigue. Remembering the extraordinary effort required to launch your *original* products may discourage you from launching *new* products.

Timing. It is hard to know whether a competitor will get to market before you or whether market demands will shift by the time your product is ready for launch.

Underlying Values

Service. Meeting market needs gives your business a reason to exist. Only sell products that help communities flourish. Refuse to profit from destructive products. – 1 Peter 4:10

Innovation. Crafting better solutions engages both creator and consumer (see chapter 5). – Exodus 31:3

Alignment. Make sure your new products fit well with your company identity.

HOW?

Steps to Implement

Examine the uniqueness of your current products. What unique solutions do you provide for your customers? As discussed in the chapter (6) on branding, why do people buy from you? Would your company leave a gaping hole of unmet needs if it suddenly vanished? If these questions expose your products and services as merely average, then perhaps you should redesign them as we outline below.

Find your focus. In keeping with your vision, mission, values, and branding, what core products and services do you want to be known for? In chapter 2, I referenced Jim Collin's "hedgehog" concept – the one thing you can be best in the world at – found where your strengths intersect the needs of the world. This is your economic engine. "While it's tempting to try to be everything to everyone, one of the most impactful ways to stand out in a crowded marketplace is to one thing well" (Hamish Campbell, Entrepreneur Magazine, August 2015, p.46). Tree

Work Now Inc does exactly that – tree work – nothing more. We've resisted being pulled into lawn care, pest control, land clearing, or debris hauling. We only prune and remove trees (especially when dead, dangerous, or invasive). For a time we did our own stump grinding, a service that customers expect from us. But we found it diverted time, equipment, and focus from our more central, more profitable work. So we subcontracted to others. Focusing on what you do best and most profitably prevents you from diluting your company identity, and draining away people, capital, and equipment. If the new product you decide to launch is vastly different than what you currently offer, consider whether a separate division (with distinct marketing) or a separate company (with distinct branding) would best serve both the old and the new.

Choose your long-term growth trajectory. Will your current business model sustain long-term growth? Will you grow by developing new products or bringing existing products to new markets, or by capturing a bigger chunk of your existing market? As mentioned in chapter 7, if the demographic and geographic scopes of your target mark are very narrow, then you'll need a wider range of products and services to keep growing your company over time. If you do decide to diversify your products or services, the following steps suggest how to go about it. Or maybe in the style of Bo Burlingham's <u>Small Giants</u>, you may choose to limit growth to focus on other priorities inside and outside your company.

Decide what type of new product or service to launch. Best case scenario is that you're creating something that your existing customers have been asking for. Or maybe it's an idea that will solve a problem your target market has.

Develop a "minimum viable product." "A minimum viable product allows you to test, collect feedback from customers and then invest the time and money necessary to make a finished product (Entrepreneur Magazine, August 2012, p.50). Without wasting a lot of time and money, this will give you quick feedback on whether you can produce something people want.

Gather tons of customer feedback. Ask them everything! And keep asking. How would they improve its: aesthetics, simplicity, functionality, durability, colors, ease of use, and materials (cost, source, environmental impact)? Record their feedback and research the cost in time and money of their best suggestions.

See if it sells at a profitable price. How many people are eager to part with cash for what you're offering? Will customers buy it at a price which includes a healthy profit margin? Sell to people outside of your friends and family to gauge the true demand for your new prototype. Will it sell at least as good as your current products? Perhaps this new launch will lead to changing your focus to a more profitable product line.

Fund it. Once developed, can you produce it in a cost-effective manner based on the prices you've been able to get? If so, figure out how to fund its research, development, and production. Don't underestimate the cost of launching a new product or service. Not accounting properly for this can kill your cash flow. In fact, growing too fast is a leading cause of business failure. A new product or location can actually divert funds from the core business, so be sure to protect your core business! On the positive side, diversifying your product lines can reduce risk if demand for your existing lines fluctuates a lot.

Perfect it with customer feedback. Using the input you gathered from customers, refine your "minimum viable product or service." Spend the time and money to get it right. Then design efficient production systems to roll it out – see the next chapter.

Case Study

"Rather than invest months of time and resources to perfect their watch, Modify Watches created a few samples in a matter of weeks that were good enough to test their concept in the marketplace. After receiving feedback from early customers, they then spent 12 months and about $70,000 of their own money to improve the quality of their watch, adding requested features such as water resistance and an alternate face size" (Entrepreneur Magazine, August 2012, p.50).

Leading Self, Employees, Systems

SELF – As keeper of the brand, decide which product ideas belong here.

EMPLOYEES – Since employees make, deliver, and collect feedback on your products and services, they are important people to listen to as you launch or relaunch products.

SYSTEMS – Write dwon the right steps you'll take to: make prototypes, collect feedback, refine final products, secure funding, and cross-sell new products to existing customers.

NOW WHAT?

Summary

Examine your products and services to see if they're providing unique solutions that people want. See if your existing and potential products align with your vision, mission, values, and branding. If new products represent your best growth strategy, make sure they strengthen rather than detract from your company focus. Test the market with quick prototypes before spending the time and money to tweak the quality. Involve your customers and employees in the design process. Make sure funding the new initiative doesn't choke your existing cash flow.

Application Questions

1. Which of your current products need to be redesigned?
2. What can you do to align existing and potential products with your company identity and focus?
3. What new products would best meet needs your existing customers have?
4. What will your "minimum viable product" be like?
5. How will you quickly test your "minimum viable product" in the market?
6. How will you fund your new product development without crippling your cash flow?

Recommended Reading

<u>New Product Development for Dummies</u> by Robin Karol and Beebe Nelson

CREATE UNIQUE CUSTOMER SOLUTIONS

Make it Happen!

What ideas has this chapter stirred in me?

What new light does this chapter shine on my leadership and my business?

What changes do I plan to make?

My actions to *Make it Happen!*	Completion dates	
	Proposed	Actual

Chapter 10 | Produce Efficiently

By Evan Keller

WHAT?

Definition

Production is how your company adds value to raw materials to create what customers want. Whether you manufacture a product or deliver a service, you can benefit from "lean" principles which originated at Toyota and have quickly been accepted worldwide as best practices to efficiently deliver what customers want, on time, and right the first time.

Expert Quote

"In highly simplified terms, efficiency concerns the cost of input for the output produced – in other words, the best use of resources and the least waste of time and effort (Christopher

Hann, "The Art of Efficiency," Entrepreneur Magazine, July 2013, p.68).

Assessment Questions

1. What steps in your production add no value to the final product – from the customer's perspective?
2. Which type of waste (time, materials, space, etc) represents your biggest opportunity to improve?
3. Do you have a culture of continuous improvement?

WHY?

Benefits

Less waste. Efficient production systems waste fewer raw materials and cause less unwanted by-products (such as pollution).

Employee involvement. When you ask employees to help improve productivity, their creative problem-solving skills kick in. When they contribute to real decisions, their sense of responsibility and ownership grows.

Customer satisfaction. They like getting what they want when they want it.

Profit. If you can do more with less, there's more fruit for your labor.

Barriers

Resistance to change. Older companies have a harder time accepting new ways of doing things. A culture of constant learning and growing requires cultivation.

Lack of margin. When you're scrambling to get everything done within your inefficient system, it's hard to find the time to improve the system. That vicious cycle perpetuates.

Lean manufacturing is counter-intuitive. "Having extra stock on hand, minimizing the number of setups, and starting jobs as early as possible seem like good practices and are done with the best of intentions, but they are deadly harmful to your overall efficiency." (http://www.mikeonmanufacturing.com/mike-on-manufacturing/2009/12/how-a-small-business-can-use-lean-manufacturing.html)

Underlying Values

Efficiency. If you don't add value in a cost-effective way, you'll be out of business soon.

Constant learning. Ongoing training of employees and ongoing improvement of processes are central to lean manufacturing. Luke 2:52

Orderliness. Safety, sanity, and stewardship require an orderly workplace. – 1 Corinthians 14:40

HOW?

Steps to Implement

Document your current work flow. Understanding your production process and its individual steps will lead to identifying waste and continually refining your process. That's efficient production in a nutshell. It often helps to draw a process map with boxes and arrows to picture how your production process works. (See more on process mapping at:

http://nnphi.org/CMSuploads/MI-ProcessMappingOverview.pdf). In your flow chart, include:

1. Task flow – steps taken by both personnel and machines.
2. Material flow – where raw materials enter, exit, and stop along the way.
3. Information flow – operating instructions and key indicators.
4. Traffic flow – movement in, around, and between workstations.

Identify waste in your production system. Lean manufacturing looks for seven types of waste:

1. Waste of overproducing – producing components that are neither intended for stock, nor planned for sale immediately.

2. Waste of waiting – refers to the idle time between operations.

3. Waste of transport – moving material more than necessary.

4. Waste of processing – doing more to the product than necessary, and more than the customer is willing to pay for.

5. Waste of inventory – excess stock of either raw materials, work in process, or finished goods.

6. Waste of motion – any motion that is not necessary to the completion of an operation.

7. Waste of defects and spoilage – defective parts that are produced and need to be reworked.

http://www.cincom.com/pdf/CM080211-3.pdf

Practice "continuous improvement." This lean concept is a translation of the Japanese "Kaizen," meaning "change (kai) for the good (zen)." This mindset of persistently pursuing perfection is important to implementing lasting change. It can keep your employees challenged and keep your company competitive. Below are a few aspects of production to keep improving.

Find the best suppliers. Since raw materials are likely amongst your highest costs, it's important to find and build strong relationships with the best suppliers. Ask yourself:

1. Can the vendor supply the needed quantity of materials at a reasonable price?
2. Is the quality good?
3. Is the vendor reliable (will materials be delivered on time)?
4. Does the vendor have a favorable reputation?
5. Is the vendor easy to work with?

(http://catalog.flatworldknowledge.com/bookhub/7?e=collins-ch11_s03)

Practice "just-in-time" inventory management. Acquire only as much raw materials as you need. This reduces your costs significantly and reduces chaos in your work flow. If you get this right waiting on parts doesn't delay your production, nor do you need lots of warehouse space to store raw materials. Just-in-time inventorying leaves less margin for error and requires having reliable suppliers nearby. This underscores the importance of great relationships with responsive suppliers who can provide what you need when you need it, in the right quantity and quality. It requires more precision on your part as well: "There are two major control factors that will be helpful for optimizing your purchasing plan and minimizing your cost of purchasing and storing inventories of raw materials. First, determine the order quantity — the size and frequency of your orders. Second, determine the reorder point — the minimum level of inventory on-hand when you need to order new inventory." http://www.bizfilings.com/Libraries/pdfs/starting-manufacturing-business-guide.sflb.ashx

Practice "just-in-time" production. A key concept in "just-in-time" production is to "pull" (by demand) rather than "push" (by supply) the jobs through your shop. Instead of making as much as you can – and increasing excess inventory of end product – you only produce as much as your customers order. This dramatically reduces excess "work in process," which takes up space and requires extra material handling. This leads us to the most counter-intuitive advice in lean manufacturing: reduce run sizes. "Reduce your job quantities to the smallest run sizes possible, even if doing so requires many more setups. Small run sizes are easier to schedule, require less material handling, improve product quality, and shorten production times. The efficiency gains far outweigh the extra setup time." http://www.mikeonmanufacturing.com/mike-on-manufacturing/2009/12/how-a-small-business-can-use-lean-manufacturing.html

Re-organize your workplace using "5S". This is a fundamental lean tool for improving a production process:

1. Sort. Keep only necessary items in the workplace.
2. Set-in-order. Arrange items (such as tools, equipment, work stations) to promote efficient work flow.
3. Shine. Clean the work area so it is neat and tidy.
4. Standardize. Set standards for a consistently organized workplace.
5. Systematize. Maintain and review standards.

Empower employees to make improvements. Give power to the people. Toyota develops "self-directed work teams" of highly trained and skilled employees who are empowered to offer ideas, make improvements and decisions, and even stop production to make corrections. This leads to everyone's creativity being engaged rather than just perpetuating inefficient processes, which were probably designed by managers who are further from the action. Actively harvesting and implementing the best ideas from employees is key to reducing product defects and manufacturing costs.

Address bottlenecks. The least efficient step in your production process slows down the entire process, just as the slowest walker in a group slows the group as a whole. Like a river dam, water backs up behind it but only trickles out ahead of it. In production, "work in process" piles up while awaiting the slow bottleneck step, whereas workstations after the bottleneck are stalled waiting for the work to flow through. Improving efficiencies of other steps without addressing the bottleneck will not speed up overall production because bottlenecks determine the "throughput" of a supply chain. It only takes a little bit of intentionality to identify your current bottleneck as it is likely painfully obvious. The harder part is managing bottlenecks effectively. Appropriate staffing and task levelling can help with personnel bottlenecks. Preventative maintenance, customization, or replacements are common fixes for equipment bottlenecks. Eliminating a bottleneck is rarely as speedy as you'd like, so you may have to creatively manage the production schedule to minimize the bottleneck's squeeze. Once you've resolved your bottleneck, a new bottleneck will arise. Hopefully, each bottleneck is less severe than the one before it, moving you steadily towards greater efficiency and profitability.

Assess what customers value. Eliminate processes that don't add value to the end product, and for which the customer is unwilling to pay. It's easy to assume that each step in your process is necessary and adds value, but companies that "go lean" are amazed and how many non-value-added components they find in their processes and products. The key to this is the customer's perspective. If customers knew each step, which of those steps would they not be willing to pay for? Remove these steps and components.

Track costs. Track your cost per unit and other key indicators you find important to efficiency and profitability – which should both increase as you follow these steps. Count not only number of products produced (per period and per batch), but by-products (wanted and unwanted), and waste. Also track intangibles such as safety, quality, and customer feedback.

Case Study

Saving time has been the biggest improvement in efficiency at Inspired Bronze in recent years. Jackie and Matt Ramieri improved their tracking of employee time per production batch by using "Harvest", an online time tracking software. After being customized for their handmade bronze and pewter awards business, this software makes it easy for them to track process times for each of the following steps in making a pewter award: molding, casting, welding, chasing, patina, and mounting. Employees simply click on their iPads when they move their batch into the next stage of production. Jackie and Matt keep a close eye on whether employees are meeting or exceeding the time budgeted for each step. This helps them supervise employees and keep customers apprised of the progress of their order. They discuss progress and obstacles with employees in their weekly production meeting.

Using this software has helped them catch employees who were intentionally wasting time and has helped their good workers get better. They catch lagging projects midstream and troubleshoot solutions to get them back on schedule. In addition to helping with employee supervision, this automated tracking of process times has given them good data on the number of employee hours it takes to produce each one of their various products. With this continual refinement, they are able to give more accurate quotes for future jobs.

See lean case studies from your own industry: http://www.lean.org/common/display/?o=2650

Leading Self, Employees, Systems

SELF - Since surviving and thriving as a company is so dependent on efficiency, you need to pay close attention to it. If you raise up strong production leaders as we advise in chapter 13, through them you can keep tabs on various key indicators of the processes we've just described.

EMPLOYEES - Given natural resistance to change, it would be wise to build ownership carefully with influential employees before launching these changes. Training and continuous learning are necessary for your employees to operate these production systems effectively. While production relies heavily on systems, unengaged employees can quickly derail any good system - so remember to treat them right. See chapter 14. Recognize and reward continuous improvement to show that the production your employees do every day is important to you.

SYSTEMS - Develop a production manual for each product to aid in quality control, standardization, training, and continuous improvement. ISO (International Organization for Standardization) certification assures customers that your processes and products meet specific quality standards. "It certifies that you can accurately and consistently build the same product week after week, year after year" (TK Donle of Complete Parachute Solutions, in conversation with the author). You'll also want to ensure there is a good system of communication between those who make, sell, deliver, and follow up on the product.

NOW WHAT?

Summary

Nimble use of inventory and work flow allows you to do more with less, pleasing customers better and faster. A commitment to lean practices of waste elimination, workplace organization, employee empowerment, and continuous improvement will increase efficiency and profitability.

Application Questions

1. How efficient is your work flow? What did you learn from your production flow chart?

2. Which of the seven categories of waste do you plan to address?

3. How can you nurture a culture of "continuous improvement" amongst your employees?

4. How can you move toward "just-in-time" inventory management and production?

5. Which of the "5S" components need the most shoring up?

6. What real-time production decisions can you empower employees to make?

7. How can you gather more ideas for improvement from employees?

8. What is your current bottleneck and what will you do about it?

9. Which production steps or product components do your customers not value enough to pay for?

Recommended Reading

The Lean Six Sigma Pocket Toolbook by Michael George

Make it Happen!

What ideas has this chapter stirred in me?

What new light does this chapter shine on my leadership and my business?

What changes do I plan to make?

My actions to *Make it Happen!*	Completion dates	
	Proposed	Actual

Circle the appropriate action for each topic:

9. Create Unique Customer Solutions - *Do I provide unique solutions that people want and fit with my company identity? Do I make prototypes of new products and test them with some of my customers?*

        Maintain   Fine-Tune   Overhaul

10. Produce Efficiently - *Am I working to improve the efficiency of my production so that I can please customers better and faster?*

        Maintain   Fine-Tune   Overhaul

MY #1 FOCUS: _____

PRODUCE EFFICIENTLY

4. Sales & Service

Sell at a high margin based on trust and superior value. Reinforce both by exceeding customer expectations.

CLOSE SUFFICIENT HIGH-MARGIN SALES

Chapter 11 | Close Sufficient High-Margin Sales

By Evan Keller

WHAT?

Definition

Enough sales at the right price are essential for positive cash flow and company growth.

Expert Quote

"You don't sell what the product is; you sell what the product does" (Zig Ziglar in <u>Secrets of Closing the Sale</u>).

Assessment Questions

1. Is your revenue steadily growing?

2. Do your salespeople communicate well the value you provide and show courage when closing?

3. Does your pricing protect a healthy profit margin?

4. Do you compete primarily on price?

5. Do you follow up diligently on those who don't immediately say "yes"?

WHY?

Benefits

Survival. Without sales, you have no company.

Excellence. Paying customers hold you accountable for quality. Those competing for your sales also keep you sharp.

Mutual value. Commercial transactions should be a win-win, with both parties sensing they got a good deal. You create value in people's lives. This leads to enjoyable relationships.

Barriers

Rare skills. Good salespeople are hard to find.

Price-conscious consumers. While the customers you want care about quality, there are many who see only price.

Under-cutting competitors. These are not your true competitors. Make sure your salespeople can tactfully share how your offerings are superior.

Inferior products. If you don't believe in what you're selling, you'll lack integrity and enthusiasm as you ask others to buy.

Underlying Values

Honesty. Don't promise more than you can deliver in order to make a sale. Rather, over-deliver to win their repeat business. Go for the long-term win-win. – Proverbs 16:11

Respect. Don't resort to coercion to make a sale. High pressure makes prospects want to say "no." Respect their right to say "no" now and they may say "yes" later. – Mathew 5:37

Steadfastness. Standing by your price takes courage, but your exceptional products and reputation back you up.

HOW?

Steps to Implement

With Salespeople:

1. **Hire true salespeople.** If possible, hire people with a strong sales experience. Chapter 13 discusses developing salespeople, including a list of traits to look for.

2. **Pay salespeople on commission.** If they really have the drive to sell, they'll want the growth potential that a commission-based salary offers. Offer a short ramp-up period (its length depends on your sales cycle) of guaranteed salary until their commissions should be strong. I made the mistake of paying my first-ever "salesman" by the hour. (Remember him from chapter 7?) With his salary guaranteed, he parked himself in the office and made the world's most beautiful databases,

complete with more than you'd ever want to know about the potential clients he never did chase. Keep your commission pay structure simple and rarely pursue it. For further advice, see Joe Worth's article in Entrepreneur Magazine: http://www.entrepreneur.com/article/234008 (June 2014, p.78).

3. **Train salespeople diligently.** With so much resting on their success, have them shadow you and your best salespeople for as long as it takes to learn to communicate your value and ask courageously for the price you need to be profitable. Set the bar high by being a high-performance salesperson yourself.

With Pricing:

1. **Avoid competing on price.** As long as you're truly providing exceptional value, people may complain about your pricing, then go ahead and buy from you anyway. That's where the courage and steadfastness come in. Often you can include a value-added service instead of reducing your price. If you lower your price too much, you devalue your product and give the impression that your first price was unfair. See more in chapter 19 on negotiation. "A focus on undercutting the competition

can start a vicious cycle that destroys your profit margins. You want customers to choose you for your superior products and services, not because you're the cheapest" (Joe Worth, Entrepreneur Magazine, August 2013, p.76).

2. **Choose your pricing strategy.** Whatever approach you take to pricing, at least know what your products are costing you. Find the price at which you'd break even with this formula:

$$\text{Breakeven Point} = \frac{\text{Fixed Costs}}{\text{Price Per Unit} - \text{Variable Cost Per Unit}}$$

You may want to go over this with your accountant. While it's important to pay attention to your costs and your competition when setting your prices, we suggest you focus most on the value your clients put on your product or service. This "customer value-based pricing" strategy is explained by MIT Sloan Management Review: "Instead of asking, 'How can we realize higher prices despite intense competition?' customer value-based pricing asks, 'How can we create additional customer value and increase customer willingness to pay, despite intense competition?'" (Summer 2012, Andreas Hinterhuber and Stephan Liozu).

3. **Raise your prices slowly over time.** Customers understand that your costs are slowly increasing. What they don't understand is why they've paid the same thing for 10 straight years, and now you want to charge them double.

With Prospects:

1. **Qualify prospects.** Before you spend too much time, energy and money chasing a prospect, determine whether they have the "interest, ability, authority, and pre-disposition" to buy. (Dan Kennedy <u>No B.S. Sales Success</u> p.138-139). As your strong value proposition (among other factors) helps your market share to grow, you'll increasingly have the luxury of choosing your customers and un-choosing others which are too costly to serve – in terms of finances or frustrations. Some people will always choose the lowest available price, and those are the customers you *don't* want. If you do business with them, they'll look for things to complain about to get even more of a discount! You want customers who see the value in what you offer and are

willing to pay for it. It's your job to *create* and *communicate* that value.

2. **Establish rapport and learn all you can about what's important to them.** Genuinely seek to establish a long-term relationship, rather than just make a quick sale. This involves getting them talking about what matters to them rather than talking about yourself or your company. People want to do business with people they trust, and who understand and care about them. See more tips on this in chapter 19 on negotiation.

3. **Don't bad-mouth your competitors.** Instead, speak of what you uniquely offer. If you need make a comparison, speak of weaknesses in the industry rather than mentioning specific competitors. Norm Brodsky puts it like this: "When I compete for an account, I always ask which other suppliers the prospective customer is considering. Most prospects name the same two or three record storage companies, our major competitors. 'Those are all fine companies,' I say, 'and you're going to be happy if you choose any one of us. Of course, I think you'll be happiest with my company.' Then I talk about our strong points, taking care not to say anything negative about the other companies. To be sure, the customer occasionally includes on the list a company I don't hold in such high regard. In that case,

I simply say, 'Well, that firm isn't really a competitor of ours, but the others we compete against all the time, and they're very good. I just think we're better, and here's why.'" (Street Smarts p.115)

4. **Understand why people buy.** Ask good questions and listen well. People have their own peculiar needs to fill. I noticed when selling cars that each person was looking for something totally different: room to stow their bicycle, tight turning radius for their small parking space, back windows that roll down completely so their dogs can sniff the wind, minimal blind spots for changing lanes safely, high profile to see above the traffic, or a cup holder that fits their favorite coffee mug. Their reasons for buying rarely had to do with car features the manufacturer was listing. Jason Fried says the same: "I made the discovery that people's reasons for buying things often don't match up with the company's reason for selling them….Understanding what people really want to know – and how that differs from what you want to tell them – is a fundamental tenet of sales" (INC Magazine, March 2011, p.56-57). It also helps to know that people buy more for emotional, rather than logical reasons.

5. **Communicate your value proposition.** Share why they should buy from you – what unique value you offer.

Show how your products are good solutions to the needs they have. Educate and reassure them as needed. To avoid competing on price alone, you need to *actually* be different (and better) than your competitors, and you need to communicate that effectively in a variety of ways. "Why choose us" should be weaved throughout your message either implicitly or explicitly – as we do in the opening paragraph of www.treeworknow.com.

6. **Discern the prospect's sense of urgency.** If you can't read their body language and tone of voice, try a preliminary close, such as: "How soon were you hoping to make this purchase?" or "How do we compare so far to our competitors?"

7. **Give them options.** Instead of a 50/50 between "yes" and "no", give them two "yes" choices to choose from. This gives them a sense of control and a chance to take a smaller risk on you or go for the deluxe package.

8. **Ask for the sale.** Ask them to buy – short and simple. Then be quiet and listen. "The only closing question structure I use is the simple yes-or-yes question. Would you prefer red or blue? With or without? Pay in three or four payments?" (Dan Kennedy No B.S. Sales Success p149). If you don't get an immediate "yes", try one of these questions without being coercive:

- What do we need to do to earn your business?
- If I did what you're requesting, would you commit right now?
- What should we eliminate in order to fit your budget?
- If we set up a payment plan for you, would you buy today?
- If I lower my price, will you increase the volume of your purchase?

9. **Allow them to say "no."** Be courteous, especially if you want their business in the future. Leave the door open, making it clear what will make a deal work for you. Remember, you hope to build a long-term relationship with them.

10. **Follow up.** Be diligent to follow up later; most people don't and loose many sales they could have easily gotten.

11. **Use tactics that fit your industry and products.** Explore up-selling, cross-selling, recurring sales programs, service agreements, loss leaders, free samples, introductory offers, money-back guarantees, warrantees, and referral discounts.

Case Study

Jackie and Matt Ramieri of Inspired Bronze were tired of competing on price. Knowing their handcrafted bronze awards were far superior to what was available in the standard trophy market, they took this challenge head-on by creating a document to educate their potential customers on why their products are expensive – and worth every penny. Steinway Pianos are a lot pricier than others, but for great reasons. Jackie and Matt borrowed their idea of creating a "buyer's guide" that – in great detail and with sharp graphics – explains the superior quality of their materials and processes. This tool has helped many customers feel good about investing in custom bronze and pewter awards. You can download it at www.inspiredbronze.com.

Leading Self, Employees, Systems

SELF – Be your company's best salesperson, then model that as you train others.

EMPLOYEES – In addition to the above advice on hiring, training, and compensating salespeople, promote good teamwork between them and those responsible to keep the promises they make.

SYSTEMS – Decide which of the above sales tactics (recurring, referrals, cross-selling, upselling, etc) fit your business and build sales systems to fit.

NOW WHAT?

Summary

Find and diligently train salespeople who can communicate the value you offer and courageously ask for the prices you need. Build rapport with prospects in order to establish a long-term relationship. Listen well to what's important to them and show how your products and services uniquely meet their needs. Add value before reducing price, and avoid competing on price. Give a bare-bones and deluxe option as you ask for the sale. Be sure to follow up with those who don't initially say "yes" as you seek to build lasting relationships of trust.

Application Questions

1. Do you need to hire additional salespeople?
2. Are your salespeople motivated by their pay structure?
3. How will you train your salespeople to connect well with clients, communicate your value proposition, and close sufficient sales at the right price?
4. What are the most common reasons people buy from you?
5. Do you need to change what you say about your competitors?
6. How will you adjust your pricing strategy?
1. What improvements should you make to your sales process?
7. Do you and your salespeople follow up well on prospects?
8. What sales tactics do you employ to increase sales to new and recurring customers?

Recommended Reading

E-Myth Mastery by Michael Gerber

Make it Happen!

What ideas has this chapter stirred in me?

What new light does this chapter shine on my leadership and my business?

What changes do I plan to make?

My actions to *Make it Happen!*	Completion dates	
	Proposed	Actual

Chapter 12 | Multiply Happy Customers

By Evan Keller

WHAT?

Definition

Exceeding customer expectations every day is essential to increasing repeat business, referrals, and building a reputation for excellence. Consistently providing extraordinary client care is the surest path to revenue growth.

Expert Quote

"The Values Institute identified five values that influence trust in a brand: **ability** (company performance); **concern** (care for consumers, employees, and community); **connection** (sharing consumer's values); **consistency** (dependability of products/services); and **sincerity** (openness and honesty)."

(Paula Andruss, "Secrets of the 10 Most-Trusted Brands," Entrepreneur Magazine, April 2012, p.55

http://www.entrepreneur.com/article/223125).

Assessment Questions

1. Do you do the right thing even when it hurts?
2. Do you know what customers want most from you?
3. What percentage of your customers tell others to buy from you?
4. How do customers rate your company compared to others?

How do you ensure your team consistently exceeds customer expectations?

WHY?

Benefits

Competitive advantage. Genuine care for every customer can set you apart from competitors and nurture a stellar reputation.

Respect. Being known for quality and excellence will elicit honor from your community.

Long-term profit. Making customers happy is good for business.

Appreciation from customers. Most will notice and thank you for taking good care of them. Mutual good feelings from a positive experience lay the foundation for a trusting relationship – maybe even a true friendship.

Barriers

Impatience. It may seem inefficient to make the extra effort to exceed customer expectations. But this can win over some customers you've disappointed, who often become your biggest advocates. Short-term inefficiency to please customers often is worth it in the long-run.

Short-term profit. As we drive so hard to sell and complete orders, we can unwittingly undercut our care for the people paying our bills.

Disengaged employees. If your employees don't enjoy their jobs, it will show in how they treat your customers. See chapter 14.

Defensiveness. It's easy to get caught up in the emotions when your customers complain – especially when they are unreasonable, exaggerate the problem, get angry, make crazy demands, refuse to pay, threaten to tell everyone and not pay, and fail to see all you do to please them.

Underlying Values

Excellence. Your team will have more pride in what they do when giving their best. – Colossians 3:23

Purpose. Meeting people's needs through goods and services is central to the purpose of business. – Mathew 6:11

Relationships. People matter. Some people won't be happy no matter what you do, but treating even those folks fairly is the right thing to do. – Ephesians 4:32

Sincerity. Be open and honest about your mistakes. Admit them, taking full responsibility for problems caused by your employees, subcontractors, suppliers, and products. Own, don't rent, the problem. – James 5:16

Empathy. When you or your employees fail, say you're sorry. Feel their pain. Listen well. Show that you care.

HOW?

Steps to Implement

Make your employees happy! Are you surprised that this is the first step? I used to be customer-centric without being employee-centric. Big mistake – my biggest one yet, actually! We must pursue employee happiness as much as customer happiness. It took me 10 years to realize that if I make my employees happy, they'll make my customers happy. Of course! Employees are happy when they have real authority, find purpose in their work, feel adequately rewarded and invested in. See more on engaging employees in chapter 14.

Ingrain customer-centric thinking into your company culture. Your vision, mission, values, and goals should constantly remind your employees that customers come first, that all of your livelihoods depend on making them happy. Our vision at Tree Work Now Inc is to "be the most trusted tree experts." Our core value of "wowing" customers has this caption: "We apply excellence and thoroughness to our work as expressed in our motto: 'Every Detail, Every Time.'" This tagline spurs us to exceed our customer expectations – even at the end of a long, hard day. "Consider the world from your prospects' point of view: How does what you sell improve their lives, shoulder their burdens, and ease their pain? Remember, your value is not in what you do. Your value is in what you do for others" (Ann Handley, Entrepreneur Magazine, May 2013, p.68).

Create and enforce customer service systems. Step-by-step processes can guide employees through how you want them to interact with customers. Include a process for unhappy customers. This process should include a way for them to talk to a manager or yourself. Train employees to use these systems and make sure they do. See more on customer service systems in chapter 4.

Offer a guarantee and deliver on it. This is an effective type of customer service system. "A guarantee is your opportunity to pinpoint an industry-wide problem and solve it. This is typically a service or quality problem. You must determine what your customers can count on from you. If you guarantee it, that will put their minds at ease and enable you to make new sales.…Your guarantee has a secondary benefit. It forces all the people in your organization to deliver on it. That in turn forces you to look inward and make sure you've got all the right people, processes, and systems in place to do so. If not, you'll be forced to improve upon it." (Wickman p.64) Below is our guarantee. The key to keeping our "Property Promise" is that our leadership team had a voice in refining it and explaining it to our crews.

1. Prevent Damage

    a. Estimator communicates with customer regarding sensitive aspects of the property.

    b. Crew leader communicates the above information to each member of the tree crew.

    c. Crew relocates whatever can be moved out of the drop zone.

    d. Crew creates a plan to minimize damage using the best techniques and access routes.

    e. Crew leaves lightest possible footprint with well-maintained, low-impact equipment.

    f. These steps are carried out by drug-free, highly experienced tree workers.

2. Repair Promptly

   a. Notify customer immediately (when possible) of any significant damage.

   b. Make repairs immediately whenever possible.

   c. Notify field maintenance coordinator who involves any necessary contractors on next business day at the latest.

   d. Office provides customer with regular updates on progress of repairs.

   e. Estimator calls to ensure customer satisfaction.

   f. Customer pays only after restoration is complete.

Differentiate your company through superior service. Especially if you sell the same products as others, you've got to add value with far superior service. Otherwise, you'll have to compete primarily on price, and you know what a death trap that is (from previous chapter). Tell them what they can expect when buying from you, then keep your promises.

Find out what customers really want. Don't assume. Ask. Tree Work Now's online submission form asks every customer what is most important to them. Then we create production systems (such as the Property Promise above) to deliver on their most frequently occurring answers.

Manage customer expectations. While most businesses try to please every customer, there are limits to what a business can do well. Being uninformed about certain trade-offs between quality, speed, and price, some customers have extremely unrealistic expectations when they first interact with you. But with a little education from you, most will adjust their expectations. Run from those who do not! There are customers you cannot afford to serve. These unhappy and unreasonable people will drain your resources and time from other customers you could be serving. Don't set yourself up to fail!

Exceed customer expectations. Once you commit to a customer, meeting expectations is not enough. Provide a memorable experience by delivering amazing products in a thoughtful, personal way. Promise big – deliver bigger!

Model and celebrate excellent customer service. Show employees how to take care of customers. And reward them when they do. We open every company meeting and leadership team meeting with recent customer testimonials of how we made them happy.

When you fail customers, go beyond what is required to fix it. Strangely enough, this can turn angry customers into your biggest advocates! It happened to me – read the case study below. Be willing to lose money in such cases – but only for those you've truly, spectacularly failed. Beware of customers who blow a minor mistake out of proportion to get something for nothing. A small percentage make a career out of being unhappy, but win over the vast majority and you'll build an army of advocates that tell all their friends.

Here's how Jason Fried, CEO of 37 Signals put it: "Of course, all companies experience episodes like this. How they handle the situation is what counts. I'm not talking about fixing the problem—you have to fix it; that's a given. I'm talking about how you communicate with your customers, how you accept responsibility, and how you make things right. That's what people remember. I've been a customer of companies that don't know how to respond to a crisis. These outfits don't own up to the problem. They hedge, they tiptoe, and they get their PR departments to issue abstract non-apology apologies. Here's one of the worst: 'We apologize for any inconvenience we may have caused.' If ever there was a nonapology apology, this is it. And just about every company uses it. I Googled the phrase *We apologize for any inconvenience*. It came up 41 million times" (Inc Magazine, February 2011, p.37. See link to full article below in Recommended Reading.)

When customers are frustrated, what they need is empathy from a fellow human. Our friend Angela Karum shares a script with people like me who need coaching in empathy. It goes like this: "I understand why you feel that way. If I was in your shoes, I would feel the same way." That simple human touch is a powerful diffuser.

Guard your reputation. It's all you have! Neither the most brilliant branding, nor the cleverest marketing can undo a tarnished reputation. It lowers the value of all a company's assets. Wells Fargo knows this well. After being a company that had achieved greatness by some standards (including being one of Jim Collins' "good to great" companies), their reputation plummeted after it was discovered that employees had opened fake accounts for millions of customers that results in millions of dollars in fees. Their stage coach logo captures our imagination of America's wild West, but trampling their customers has negated any positive feelings their branding had conjured.

Conversely, a reputation for excellence is better than any advertising that money can buy.

Get feedback from as many customers as possible. How you do this depends on what kind of business you have and how you connect with customers. We contact every customer to see how we did and how we can improve.

Give them ways to share. We ask for referrals in a note thanking them for their business and reward them for referring their friends. We ask for Google reviews (also Angie's List and BBB) and post other testimonials on our website. We ask them to recommend us to their neighbors on nextdoor.com.

Use feedback to improve the customer experience. Identify the most frequent complaints and make the necessary changes. Make product improvements, replace or retrain unfriendly staff, make your ordering and billing processes faster or friendlier – whatever it takes.

Case Study

"When I needed to have tree work done on my property, I called Tree Work Now to provide a quote for the work that was needed. After meeting with owner Evan Keller I felt confident in his sincerity and willingness to provide the best service possible. For this reason I chose them to provide that service.

The team for the most part did an excellent job, but because of a miscommunication between Evan and his team, one of the trees near the house was heavily over-pruned. When arriving home that day I immediately called Evan and he came right over to assess the situation. Because the tree in question was near the house, he understood why the team took the action that they did, but acknowledged that it was not at all what we had discussed. Evan took full responsibility for the error, and in his willingness to earn my complete satisfaction, he allowed me to make the decision of how to compensate for this error, even leaving me the option of not paying ANYTHING for the full day's work his company had rendered!

Evan's handling of this matter was so professional that when I again needed tree work done I chose Tree Work Now. This time the work that was necessary was very difficult because one of the large trees that needed to be removed was completely surrounded by hardscape. The team did an excellent job and I could not have been happier with the results.

In the future when I need tree service again, there will be no question whom I will use. I highly recommend Evan and his team because of their skill, integrity, and professionalism." – Barry Smith, Deland, Florida

Leading Self, Employees, Systems

SELF – Center your company on customers. If all you talk about is sales, finance, and production, your employees will take the cue that customers are secondary.

EMPLOYEES – Make sure your people who deal with customers have people skills are have been trained in your customer-centric values and systems. And remember to be employee-centric too – like making their voice count, providing an attractive career path with training and responsibilities to develop toward it, and show them regularly that you really care about them as people, not just what they can do for you. I was surprised to learn that even the big burly men that work for me really need a hug and a kind word from me.

SYSTEMS – Processes for lead generation, sales, client fulfilment, and follow up should all be designed to exceed customer expectations.

NOW WHAT?

Summary

Make extraordinary customers care part of your company's identity – modelling, training, and implementing systems that help your employees exceed customer expectations. When your employees fail a customer, take responsibility and show empathy as you make things right. Follow up with customers to continually improve their experience. Your team will take pride in providing excellent value and your customers will return and bring their friends.

Application Questions

1. How can pleasing customers be worked into your foundational documents and company culture?
2. What stories of winning over customers should become part of your company lore?
3. Are there any disgruntled customers you should to attempt to win over?
4. What customer-focused systems do you need to build, improve, or better implement?
5. How can you celebrate and reward extraordinary customer care?
6. How can you get more feedback from customers?

Recommended Reading

"How to Turn Disaster into Gold" by Jason Fried, CEO of 37 Signals, Inc. Magazine, February 2011:

http://www.inc.com/magazine/20110201/how-to-turn-disaster-into-gold.html

Make it Happen!

What ideas has this chapter stirred in me?

What new light does this chapter shine on my leadership and my business?

What changes do I plan to make?

My actions to *Make it Happen!*	Completion dates	
	Proposed	Actual

Circle the appropriate action for each topic:

11. Close Sufficient High-Margin Sales - *Do I build trusting relationships with my potential customers, communicating the value I offer and standing firm on my prices?*

                Maintain   Fine-Tune   Overhaul

12. Multiply Raving Fans - *Do I consistently exceed my customers' expectations and go beyond what is required to fix my customer mistakes?*

                Maintain   Fine-Tune   Overhaul

MY #1 FOCUS: _____

5. Employees

Multiply your capacity by raising up leaders with real authority. Create a win-win by helping employees grow their skills and build their teamwork. Show them a path for advancement, and that you care.

Chapter 13 | Hire & Delegate to Leaders

By Evan Keller

WHAT?

Definition

If you merely want a job, keep all major responsibilities to yourself. But if you want a sustainable company, you must develop others to fill key roles, so you can focus on leading long-term growth.

Expert Quote

"When selecting someone, [great managers] select for talent…not simply experience, intelligence, or determination. When setting expectations, they define the right outcomes…not the right steps. When motivating someone, they focus on strengths…not on weaknesses. When developing someone, they help him find the right fit…not simply the next rung on the ladder" (Marcus Cunningham and Curt Coffman, <u>First, Break All the Rules</u> p.67).

Assessment Questions

1. Which of your current roles do you think no one else can fill? What do you base this assessment on?
2. Is your current workload sustainable?
3. Would your company survive if you died today?

WHY?

Benefits

Focus on innovation. When others are keeping daily operations going, you can focus your creative energy on charting the future, increasing sales, launching new initiatives, building systems, and leading well. You can see the big picture and do some of the "not-urgent-but-important" work suggested in this book.

Increased company value. Your company is a lot more valuable to potential buyers if it runs well without your full-time effort. Buyers want a company that retains a high capacity after you are gone.

Sanity. It can be lonely and overwhelming when you're the only one tackling your business challenges. When others share that burden, both your workload and your stress load are more manageable.

Free time. You have some margin in your life for relationships, interests, and service.

Barriers

Martyr complex. Some would lose their sense of identity if they weren't always over-busy. Those who work too much, crave sympathy for always being stressed out. This is unsustainable, like "driving a 200 km per hour in first gear" (Lee Murray, overheard mentoring entrepreneurs in Haiti).

Self-importance. Some entrepreneurs need to be needed. It seems odd and humbling when employees know more about certain aspects of your business than you do! Swallow your pride, learn from them, help them succeed, and be grateful that your enterprise has grown into something bigger than yourself. Phil Libin, CEO of Evernote lives by this rule: "Everyone who reports to me has to be much better at doing his or her job than I could ever be" (INC Magazine, March 2013, p.26).

Technician mentality. "It's easier to do it myself" rather than train someone else to do it right. You may have started your business because you love the work, but as we repeat this again and again, hopefully you now see that it's more important to become a leader. If no employee can complete a particular task as well as you can, that's not something to be proud of. To the contrary, it's your fault that you haven't trained, modelled and coached them towards competence.

Control. For some, it boils down to being a controlling person. Or they fear raising up future competitors. This sense of insecurity refuses to share power or rejoice when others succeed.

Lack of qualified candidates. Most entrepreneurs I know would make more hires immediately if they could find the right people. Good people are hard to find – and keep.

Underlying Values

Trust. You've got to learn to let go. Your business won't grow much if you refuse to entrust real responsibility to others. Either provide opportunities for employees to earn the trust necessary for greater responsibility or find new employees who are more trustworthy. – Exodus 18:13-26

Synergy. Whereas all the initiative and ideas used to come from you, you'll begin to see employees make important contributions and hopefully spur each other on to innovate. – Romans 12:3-8

Growth. Both your company and your employees will grow as you develop leaders.

Dignity. People are not machines to do your dirty work. They've been given abilities that you have partial responsibility to develop.

HOW?

Steps to Implement

Look ahead. Decide what leadership roles will need to be in place long-term in order to significantly advance your vision and mission. Plan backwards to decide which positions you'll need to create in the short-term. If you'll eventually need a sales *manager* and an office *manager*, start with hiring a sales*person* and an office *worker*.

Define your own role. Decide what your company most needs from you and engages your strengths. Then you'll see which role to pass on. But first, here's a word of caution that may pop your paradigm: "Whatever is the strength of a leader often becomes the weakness of the organization (ie: if the founder is strong in marketing, the business may eventually find it's weak in this functional area). Why? Because leaders have a tendency to hold on too tight, strangling the efforts of those around them. Or the leaders figure they can "watch over the details," bringing in someone too junior to oversee the function vs. bringing in the powerhouse they really need. Instead, leaders must make a counterintuitive decision and find people who exceed their own capabilities in their area of strength, to prevent the company from stalling" (Harnish p.47).

Check the budget and plan ahead. Figure out whether there is cash flow or reserves to cover additional payroll. How long will it take for the added efficiencies or revenue they generate to cover their salaries?

Identify candidates. Look for current employees to fill those roles, if possible, to build on existing trust and expertise. Identify outside candidates, if necessary, tapping your personal network first for people your associates can recommend. Advertisement and employment agencies can also identify candidates.

Look for these top 10 traits in salespeople and sales managers:

1. Are driven and determined.
2. Engage easily in conversation.
3. Know when and how to listen carefully.
4. Can read people well, quickly perceiving customers' motives, values, and level of urgency.
5. Exude a contagious enthusiasm.

6. Build rapport and trust quickly.

7. Are likeable.

8. Are able to communicate your product's value.

9. Have courage ask for the sale and stick with their price.

10. Remain positive even when rejected repeatedly.

Look for these top 10 traits in production managers:

1. Are linear thinkers who can easily break down a process into a logical, efficient sequence.

2. Constantly look to reduce waste and increase efficiency.

3. Can handle complexity; can coolly multi-task.

4. Are good at motivating employees.

5. Are good and empathetic communicators.

6. Can train and coordinate others to accomplish tasks.

7. Care about safety.

8. Care about quality and give attention to detail.

9. Are responsible.

10. Work through adversity to get things done.

Look for these top 10 traits in office managers:

1. Are adept at multi-tasking.
2. Are detail-oriented.
3. Are task-oriented.
4. Are responsible with money, bills, and deadlines.
5. Are savvy with technology.
6. Have bookkeeping skills.
7. Are good at communicating with customers, employees, and suppliers.
8. Exude positivity.
9. Are trustworthy.
10. Can quickly provide various team members with the information they need to succeed.

Use experience-based interview questions. To find out if they have the above traits, ask questions that simulate hypothetical situations ("what would you do if…?") and questions that recall real-life experiences ("tell us about a time when…").

Use assessments to gauge aptitudes. Use tools such as StrengthsFinder and DISC to learn what your candidates are good at and what their default ways of working and relating are. Use these tools to ensure you get the "right people in the right seats on the bus," something Jim Collins (in <u>Good to Great</u>) says is essential to building a great company.

Hire people with general leadership ability. In addition to the role-specific traits above, Bill Hybels suggests looking for these general traits in a potential leader: "influence, character, people skills, drive, and intelligence." He also suggests making your own top five list (<u>Courageous Leadership,</u> p.130).

Don't make questionable hires. As the wise proverbs says "hire slow, fire fast" implies, you'll avoid many headaches and much expense by getting the hire right, even if it takes a long time to find the right person. Jim Koch (founder and chairman of Boston Beer) says: "We've had jobs that have been open for as long as a year and a half, looking for the right person. The simple rule is, never hire somebody who doesn't raise the average. If they aren't improving your company, then why would you hire that person? My worst mistakes have been what I think of as desperation hires" (INC Magazine, November 2015, p.120). "Research strongly suggests that you need a minimum of 20 applicants per position if you want to dramatically increase your odds of hiring A players." But what if you can't find that many qualified applicants? Verne Harnish continues his good advice:

"The marketing team must be as actively involved in recruiting a steady stream of potential employees as it is in attracting potential customers" (Harnish p.62).

Have new hires shadow you first. Modelling is the best way to develop leaders. You cannot expect anything from emerging leaders that you're not willing to do yourself. Water flows downhill. Let them see how you do things and how you think – especially when crisis hits. "For emerging leaders to become seasoned, wise, and effective leaders, they need proximity to and interaction with veteran leaders" (Bill Hybels, Courageous Leadership p.132).

Set them up to succeed. Provide a clear job description and share your top expectations. Be intentional about their training. Give them systems to follow that demonstrate how you've done it in the past – then get their ongoing input to improve those processes. See chapter 4.

Use "situational leadership" to prepare them for increasing responsibility. "Directing, coaching, supporting, and delegating" are four progressive steps in leading a maturing employee. At first, the employee needs "specific directions about roles and goals." In the coaching and supporting phases, the employee is given lots of feedback and is encouraged to share in the decision-making process. When trust has been properly built, "the leader empowers the employee to act independently with appropriate resources to get the job done" ("Creating Effective Leaders Through Situational Leadership," Blanchard Training and Development, Inc. https://www.theseus.fi/bitstream/handle/10024/33027/Mwai_Esther.pdf?sequence=2).

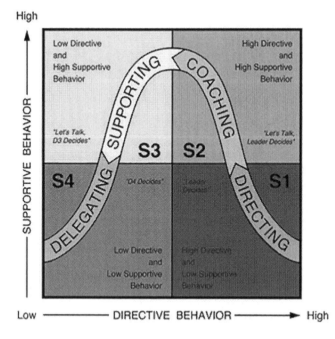

Give them real responsibility and authority. You can start small when testing an existing employees' leadership potential, but their leadership abilities will only truly mature when given challenging opportunities. If you give them a measure of autonomy, they will grow in confidence as decision-makers and will have a stronger sense of ownership in their roles. Captain David Marquet utilized this concept to turn the worst performing submarine in the US Navy's fleet into the top performing sub – in only two years' time! "Instead of one captain giving orders to 134 men, we would have 135 independent, energetic, emotionally committed and engaged men thinking about what we needed to do and ways to do it right. This process turned them into active leaders as opposed to passive followers." In <u>Turn the Ship Around!</u>, he advises: "Don't move information to authority, move authority to the information" (p.49. He then addresses the fears that keep entrepreneurs from delegating decisions to their employees: "I usually find that the worries fall into two broad categories: issues of competence and issues of clarity. People are worried that the next level down won't make good decisions, either because they lack the technical competence about the subject or because they don't understand what the organization is trying to accomplish. Both of these can be resolved" (p.58-59).

Case Study

Cereste (bottom left) appointed his cousin (bottom middle) Wilson to be production manager over the bakery he'd run himself for several years in Leogane, Haiti.

This freed up Cereste to grow his salesforce – street vendors – who sold his "pomket" muffins to drivers and pedestrians all over town. In a matter of months, he was able to more than double his salesforce to 27! Two years later, he'd grown as a leader and businessman to the point that he was able to successfully launch a second bakery (below) – one that made traditional bread. He soon trained a manager to share the responsibility. By developing leaders, he was able to create 12 jobs overnight in one of the world's most challenging economic environments!

Leading Self, Employees, Systems

SELF – Although you had to do everything when starting your business, ask yourself what you're truly best at, what you enjoy, and what your company needs most from you. Overcome your fear of letting go of roles others can do well.

EMPLOYEES – Talk about "our" company – a small but important way of saying their contributions matter. Provide new challenges to keep them engaged, and ongoing training to grow their capacity.

SYSTEMS – Show new hires how they can progress professionally, increasing their salary along with their responsibility. Avoid losing good people because they see no opportunity to advance."

NOW WHAT?

Summary

You may find it hard to delegate roles you've filled from the very start of your business. This mental and emotional inability to let go and trust others can sabotage your company's growth. So, decide what sales, production, and office roles to fill and what temperaments and talents are most important in them. Next, find and assess good candidates, then develop and support these new leaders, with access to you and real responsibility being the most critical predictors of their growth. This will allow you to invest your time more strategically in growing your company.

Application Questions

1. What in you may be sabotaging your company's growth (see "Barriers" above)?
2. What are some roles you'd like to pass on in the next 12 months? How would you prioritize these?
3. What would be the best reassignment of your own time that is freed up?
4. Who within your company can you develop into a leader?
5. Which leadership positions do you need to make outside hires to fill? How will you find good candidates?
6. Who are well-connected, trusted friends who may know quality candidates they could refer to you?
7. What qualities do you value most in the leadership roles you need to fill?
8. What tools will you use to assess candidates?
9. How will you develop your new leaders?

Recommended Reading

<u>Now, Discover your Strengths</u> by Marcus Cunningham and Donald Clifton

Make it Happen!

What ideas has this chapter stirred in me?

What new light does this chapter shine on my leadership and my business?

What changes do I plan to make?

My actions to *Make it Happen!*	Completion dates	
	Proposed	Actual

Chapter 14 | Engage Employees

By Evan Keller & Jennifer Pettie

WHAT?

Definition

"Employee engagement is the emotional commitment the employee has to the organization and its goals." When employees care about their work and their company, they willingly give their discretionary effort – going above and beyond their job description.

(Kevin Kruse, author of Employee Engagement 2.0: http://www.forbes.com/sites/kevinkruse/2012/06/22/employee-engagement-what-and-why/).

Expert Quote

"Good leaders create prosperity, and it's not defined just by money, but by the emotional health of their employees. Good leaders treat employees as humans and appreciate them by creating an environment people want to be in. Good leadership creates happy employees, who create happy customers and, ultimately, happy shareholders." – Tasha Eurich, author of Bankable Leadership as quoted in Entrepreneur Magazine May 2014.

Assessment Questions

1. Who is your all-time best employee and why? Which actions of yours increased or decreased his/her engagement?

2. Do your employees work like they care about your company? How would you describe their attitudes towards their jobs?

3. How consistently do your employees recommend your company as a place to work and a place to do business?

WHY?

Benefits

Less: turnover, murmuring, accidents, wasted time, wasted materials, and friction between employees and employers.

More: productivity, positivity, innovation, initiative in solving problems, genuine concern for the company, customer satisfaction, and commitment to company values/mission/vision.

Barriers

Lack of care. With Gallup reporting that a mere 30% of employees in the US feel engaged at work, they often sense that their employer doesn't care about them as people, but are merely using them as a tool to make money. If they don't feel cared for, they won't care about the company. They will disengage, burn out, and just go through the motions.

Out-of-touch management. Management seems aloof from the job challenges of the workforce and measures are not taken to ensure job safety and good working conditions.

Lack of Influence. Employees don't feel like their voices matter at work.

Micromanagement. Employees have no sense of autonomy or latitude to use their own problem-solving skills.

Lack of recognition. Employees don't feel appreciated.

Underlying Values

People matter. With intrinsic dignity and value, they must be treated as humans first and workers second. – Jeremiah 22:13

Invest wisely. Studies have shown that much of what you value in terms of company success depends on nurturing engaged employees. "Give, and you will receive." – Luke 6:38

Balance complementary values. The mission of your company and the people who you depend on to accomplish it are both important. While showing interest in their lives outside of work, don't shy away from calling out their best efforts on the job.

HOW?

Steps to Implement

Publicly recognize superior performance. Employees thrive on positive feedback; who doesn't? Dopamine is released in our brains whenever we hear something we like. Being valued is a primary human need, so genuine personal expressions of recognition, praise, and appreciation are considered important drivers of employee engagement. It takes only a little intentional effort, but gives big returns. In fact, Mark Twain once said "I can live for two months on one good compliment" (Maxwell, Teamwork 101, Thomas Nelson, Nashville TN 2008, p.87). It's great to encourage employees in private, but it's far more powerful when made public. You can recognize them through company awards, commendations at staff meetings, 'employee of the month' programs, newsletters, and social media or blog posts. Consistent high performance should lead to promotions and increased influence in company decisions. But don't wait for big milestones to praise good work. Rather look for ways to be encouraging every week, using your existing communication channels, hand-written notes, and thoughtful words shared face-to-face. Read customer reviews and thank you letters out loud to employees who devised solutions and gave exceptional service. "Recognizing a good idea or dedication to a project fuels engagement, particularly when it goes to a person's sense of competence, rather than just results. ('I like how you handled that'). A sense of competence is a core psychological need that drives intrinsic motivation and a continuous interest in the work at hand" (Joe Robinson in Entrepreneur Magazine May 2013 p.64).

Don't insult or shame them. Treat them right – with kindness, consideration, patience, and gratitude. They will treat your customers the way you treat them. When correcting them, do so privately and focus on specific behavior rather than making it personal. "Humans like to say they make rational decisions, but in reality they are driven by emotions, which people post-rationalize when explaining their choices to others….People personalize their job through emotions felt about the organization's actions as a whole and about their own supervisors in particular….The immediate supervisor is the chief emotional driver in the workplace; reactions to him or her explain 82% of how employees feel about their organization" (Dale Carnegie Training White Paper entitled: Emotional Drivers of Employee Engagement). While many of us would rather focus solely on tasks rather than venturing into the murky waters of "feelings", that isn't really possible. People don't leave their emotions behind, but come to work as whole people, and how they feel at work profoundly influences how they perform. You and any other supervisors in your company should avoid evoking negative emotions, and instead try to help employees feel *valued, confident, inspired, enthusiastic,* and *empowered.* The same Dale Carnegie study found these five positive emotions to be the biggest drivers of employee engagement. "Those who emotionally connect in a positive way with an organization feel a sense of ownership and are more likely to stay with it, delivering superior work in less time."

Give them a higher sense of purpose. "The first imperative involves articulating, demonstrating, and imbuing the company with a higher purpose. That purpose may relate to the work that the business does, or the way that the business does it, or the good that comes from doing it, or some combination of the three, but however you frame the higher purpose, it serves the same function. It makes the work people do meaningful; it continually reminds them how their contribution matters and why they should care about giving their best effort" (Burlingham p.110-111). A good start would be to ask your team what higher purpose their work serves. When I asked my employees, they talked about how healthy trees benefit people, how we make properties safer and more beautiful, how we develop our skills and provide for our families, and how we build positive, trusting relationships with clients who deserve better than our industry usually offers. These answers tie in with our vision ("be the most trusted tree experts") and our values ("We <u>"wow" every single customer</u>. We work to deepen relationships of trust with current and future customers." We <u>love our customers' trees</u>, finding pleasure in improving their safety, health, and beauty. We set a <u>higher standard of professionalism</u> in our industry, so that all tree companies must offer better service to Central Floridians). They may not have consciously made those connections, but it's my job to connect the dots so that their sense of purpose is reinforced. Centering your company around core values is key to infusing purpose, especially if those values focus on serving others. "People want to be a part of something bigger than themselves, something they can be proud of" (Dale Carnegie study cited above). According to Forbes, when Mark

Zuckerberg returned to Harvard (the college he 'dropped out' of to start Facebook), purpose was the theme of his commencement address: "Purpose is that sense that we are part of something bigger than ourselves, that we are needed, that we have something better ahead to work for. Purpose is what creates true happiness." That "something bigger" is often related to making a difference in the lives of people. The sense of altruism in serving others is so deeply built-in to human purpose that it trumps most other motivations – including money. For example, a blood bank wanted to increase its stock of blood, so began paying people for their blood. You can guess what happened…it backfired! Why? Because the blood bank undercut the stronger altruistic motive – helping others – that motivates many to share their blood. The blood bank snatched a high purpose and replaced it with a low one - swapped a diamond for a fake (Harvard Business Review). So, help your employees find purpose where their skills intersect the needs of the world. Make sure your company truly serves people well and makes a difference in the world.

Give them what they need to do their job. Set them up to succeed, giving them enough time, teammates, tools and training. If you create an environment in which they can achieve small successes every day, this virtuous circle positively reinforces their work and can lead to ever greater achievements. One of the 12 affirmations (see below) Gallup found in engaged employees is: "I have the materials and equipment I need to do my work right." Many entrepreneurs launch their business in an all-out 24-7 scramble to survive then achieve – and automatically expect employees to jump in beside them with the same intensity. While making their roles and responsibilities challenging, don't make them unsustainable.

GALLUP'S Q¹²*

01. I know what is expected of me at work.

02. I have the materials and equipment I need to do my work right.

03. At work, I have the opportunity to do what I do best every day.

04. In the last seven days, I have received recognition or praise for doing good work.

05. My supervisor, or someone at work, seems to care about me as a person.

06. There is someone at work who encourages my development.

07. At work, my opinions seem to count.

08. The mission or purpose of my company makes me feel my job is important.

09. My associates or fellow employees are committed to doing quality work.

10. I have a best friend at work.

11. In the last six months, someone at work has talked to me about my progress.

12. This last year, I have had opportunities at work to learn and grow.

Get rid of lazy employees. People who are lazy lower the morale and productivity of the entire team. Why should a hard-working employee have to do the work for someone else you're paying to do nothing? Poor performers are among the biggest de-motivators on a team. Before the poison spreads, gather your courage and terminate them in order to keep your hard-working employees and attract others who love to work. One of Gallup's

12 indicators of employee engagement is: "My fellow employees are committed to doing quality work."

Collect feedback and act on it. Let your employees know their concerns and ideas will be heard and respected. Employees need to know that their opinions matter. Make "your voice matters" a constant mantra. Listen well and take notes as they talk. Ask for their opinions on products, services, operational efficiency, safety, and what is needed to get the job done better. We use the below survey to get quick feedback at company meetings. Feel free to print and use it yourself. Thanks to Verne Harnish for suggesting these three simple yet powerful questions. (Harnish p.137).

> What should we...
>
> **START DOING?**
>
> **STOP DOING?**
>
> **KEEP DOING?**

While we solicit direct feedback at Tree Work Now, we recognize that some employees are hesitant to speak their mind for a variety of reasons. So, we have our "Team Builder" (who has trusting relationships with other teammates) meet quarterly with each employee, getting them to open up about their perspectives, and anonymously passes information to my brother and I who set in motion changes that need to be made.

Without positive changes, soliciting feedback can backfire and make them jaded. So, be sure to follow up with action. When you choose not to make a change they suggest, respond to their comments with appreciation and your own perspective. "This lets your staff know the company takes employee concerns seriously and cares about what they have to say" (Truist blog: http://truist.com/employee-engagement-ideas-that-work/).

Develop employees by granting responsibility and autonomy. Give them opportunities to learn and grow, helping them obtain education and training to progress in their career. As employees grow in competence and reliability, give them more freedom to do their jobs in their own way. People are more engaged when they have an opportunity to think and use their own creativity to solve problems. Imagine how low your own job satisfaction would be if you were told exactly how to do every aspect of your job every day! Even give them room for small failures and help them learn from those mistakes. A measure of autonomy – with regular debriefing – will grow their leadership capacity and job satisfaction. As their capacity and skills grow, give them ever new challenges to keep them engaged. In his book Drive, Daniel

Pink identifies three keys to employee motivation: "autonomy, mastery, and purpose."

Choose a cause and do some good. One of the most powerful ways to improve engagement is to have a company vision for community service. Employee volunteer programs increase engagement by encouraging "team building, skill development, and leadership along with the positive feelings that come from doing good" (Frontstream blog: http://www.frontstream.com/5-employee-engagement-activities-to-help-your-bottom-line/). Ask your employees what causes are important to them and their families. To make the most of community activities, offer a wide selection of opportunities to volunteer and support financially. Provide progress updates on how these community projects are succeeding and then celebrate progress.

Have fun together. Celebrate success, recognizing your team's hard work and dedication. Be intentional about scheduling time for employees to have fun. Make time during holidays or random occasions for down time with employees. This can prevent employees from burning out and shows them you value more than just work and profit. Friendships will develop; trust will deepen.

Case Study

Tree Work Now Inc has a ways to go in earning employees' discretionary effort, but we've made some good strides. We used to pack in workdays as long as the sun was up, but have realized that was a recipe for burnout, both physically (trimming trees in the hot Florida sun) and emotionally (when they rarely saw their families).

We've updated our fleet of heavy equipment so equipment failure over-extends the workday less often. We quickly terminate workers who don't want to work since they ruin team morale and productivity. We have cookouts, pool parties, scavenger hunts, deep-sea fishing and spa days to strengthen personal relationships. We increase our benefits package every six months. Even with all this, some employees don't feel appreciated because of their dangerous, hard physical work and laborers' pay. A matching savings program helps a little, and we're intentional in developing our highest capacity folks toward the higher paying roles. We can measure discretionary effort by how far that motto ("Every Detail. Every Time.") is followed in small choices throughout their workday.

While we already provide a much higher level of professionalism that is expected from our industry, we've not yet reached our own standards. We go for fairly long stretches without employee turnover, but it still comes in waves. I look forward to putting this chapter into better practice in my own business!

Leading Self, Employees, Systems

SELF – "Managers who tended to be calm, business-focused, organized and willing to listen were three times as likely to have highly engaged work groups, compared to managers described as manipulative, arrogant, distractible, and overly attention-seeking" (Rob Reuteman, *How Much Money is a Good Leader Really Worth?*" Entrepreneur Magazine, March 2014).

EMPLOYEES – Annual performance reviews are powerful tools to communicate how they are doing and give them direction in their ongoing development. These reviews are most effective when you refer to them throughout the year and implement employee development plans.

SYSTEMS – Employee awards that reinforce your company values are great ways to recognize those you catch doing something right. Implement a feedback loop so you can make changes that employees suggest.

NOW WHAT?

Summary

Engaged employees have a strong sense of loyalty to your business. They care about the company and work to further its goals. Giving their "discretionary effort" – "heart and hustle" – stems from a sense of ownership and personal connection to "our company." This elusive connection can be nurtured through some of these employer actions: showing appreciation, not demeaning, building purpose, setting up for success, terminating the lazy, acting on feedback, encouraging learning, having fun and doing service projects together.

Application Questions

1. Do you know what is important to each of your employees outside of work? Do you ask about these interests and relationships regularly?
2. How can you better communicate that you value your employees?
3. Which of the nine above steps do you need to take with your employees? Prioritize them and identify specific next steps for each.
4. How does your company rate according to Gallup's Employee Engagement Survey? (http://www.dandbconsulting.com/12-questions-to-measure-employee-engagement/)

Recommended Reading

<u>Drive: The Surprising Truth About What Motivates Us</u> by Daniel H. Pink

Make it Happen!

What ideas has this chapter stirred in me?

What new light does this chapter shine on my leadership and my business?

What changes do I plan to make?

My actions to *Make it Happen!*	Completion dates	
	Proposed	Actual

Chapter 15 | Build Teamwork

By Grace John & Mano De La Vega

Definition

Synergy amongst employees is beautiful and all too rare. True teamwork is enjoyable and spurs excellence. High performance teams produce results that are far greater than the sum of their parts, working hard, working smart, and relying on each other's strengths. This happens when you provide clarity of mission, clear expectations, and intentional development of team members and the team as a whole.

Expert Quote

"Coming together is the beginning, keeping together is progress, working together is success." – Henry Ford

(http://www.brainyquote.com/quotes/authors/h/henry_ford.html).

Assessment Questions

1. Do your employees enjoy working together? Do they spend time together outside of work?

2. Do they bring their unique strengths to the table to generate and implement good ideas?

3. Do they make each other better?

4. Do you build team synergy around adherence to your company values?

5. Do your employees know where you're taking them as a team?

6. Does your team know what tasks they perform well and what skills they need to develop further?

7. Do you give them opportunities to learn and grow?

WHY?

Benefits

Attractive culture. When teams enjoy each other and accomplish much, others want in.

High performance. As you provide training and growth opportunities, teams grow in their capacity to achieve much together.

Innovation. A strong team is energized by continuous improvement. Their creative energy is focused on making progress together.

Growth. A strong team can grow your business, serving more customers and achieving your goals faster.

Diversity. Teams bring diversity of thought, experience, education, and skillset.

Barriers

Hostile employer/employee relations. If your employees perceive that their workload is too high and their pay is too low, they will have negative attitudes that will preempt positive teamwork. If you don't care about your employees, they won't care about their jobs or teammates.

Neglect. Many entrepreneurs expect all the focus to be on the work and the customer, so they only focus on the team when there's a crisis to solve. We complain about employees who don't care, and expect smooth, productive teamwork to happen automatically. We'd have fewer team crises if we focused more on developing team members and teamwork.

Politics. Excessive drama and power struggles between employees can ruin team chemistry. So can personality conflicts. Beware of self-promoting employees whose selfishness eclipses any concern for fellow teammates and team performance.

Underperformance. If employees lack the work ethic or skills to do their share of work, they should be terminated, retrained, or reassigned. Otherwise, team morale will suffer and other teammates will underperform.

Lack of Clarity. If your team does not know and align with your vision, mission, and values, you will have individuals going in different directions. Building teamwork requires pulling individuals together to work towards common goals.

Underlying Values

Vision: When you have clarity on your mission, you can envision your team to make it a reality. – Proverbs 29:18

Sustainable workloads. Valuing results more than people produces weaker results. *How* you reach your goals matters as much as reaching them. Don't trample people to meet your goals; it's not sustainable. You must simultaneously value the team's members and mission.

Maximizing strengths. Team members' gifts need to be discovered, developed and stewarded for individual and corporate benefit. – 1 Corinthians 12:4-7

Fun. Relationships are meant to be enjoyed between people who respect each other's unique abilities.

Synergy. It is deeply satisfying to work together to create solutions that no one team member could have accomplished alone. – 1 Corinthians 12:12

HOW?

Steps to Implement

Be sure you have the right people on the team. Hire slow; terminate fast. Hire for both skills and character traits that you want in a potential employee. Technical skills can be more easily taught than traits like confidence, assertiveness, and good judgment. Don't build a team that looks, speaks, and acts all the same. Build a diverse team, as each individual's unique talent will make your team stronger, but make sure you can develop some chemistry between them. See more on hiring in chapter 13.

Assign employees to the right positions on the team. Once you have good people, make sure they have roles that fit their strengths, personalities, and capacities. When your intuition isn't enough, use assessment tools (StrengthsFinder, Meyers-Briggs, DISC) to shape job roles. Write job descriptions to clarify their roles.

Align your team with your core values. Share how your company values (as developed according to chapter 2) are an extension of your personal core values. Emphasize how important these are to you and that you expect every team member to embody these values at work. Share how serious you are about every employee adhering to these values. Demonstrate this by constantly recognizing every little adherence, disciplining for minor infractions, and terminating for major infractions. Company values are a great foundation to build your team upon. Make values the glue that binds employees together. Values set the boundaries in which the game must be played. You have to make sure your team understands what you will tolerate and what you will not tolerate in the operation of your business. If you don't enforce your values, they will act according to their own core values. Without a unifying focus, chaos and conflict will abound.

Set and achieve goals together. Ensure everyone knows your company mission (which aligns with your vision and values – see chapter 2), and develop annual and quarterly goals (see chapter 3) to advance your mission. To build ownership, get input from employees on setting these goals and the strategy for achieving them. Respect their problem-solving abilities by getting their help in breaking down three-year goals into one-year goals, and one-year goals into ninety-day key performance indicators (KPI's) that have a numerical component that shows whether or not it was accomplished. Notice how people compete harder in a game when you keep score? Numbers motivate! Short-term victories will encourage your team, and make the bigger goals seem more attainable.

Consistently reinforce your team goals: Don't share your goals just once and expect your team to magically own and accomplish them. "Vision leaks" (Andy Stanley. <u>Making Vision Stick</u>). It needs to be reinforced many times in many ways.

Set high and clear expectations. Each team member should know how you want them to move your mission and goals forward. If employees don't know what to do, they will act according to their own expectations. Your expectations should be tailored to their individual roles and strengths, so make sure each team member knows exactly what you expect from them. All or part of your expectations can be in their job descriptions, but don't let that piece of paper be the end of it – reinforce regularly. At Tree Work Now, job descriptions are condensed down into each employees top 5-9 job duties, which are listed on the company organizational chart ("Responsibility Chart") and integrated into performance reviews every six months.

Model high performance. The team will not outperform you, and needs you to set high standards of integrity. Are you a leader by title only? Consistently providing an example of excellent work is the only way to inspire your team to high performance.

Create systems for team members to follow. Written step-by-step processes remind employees how you want things done. This reinforces your expectations and helps you trust them to do things right. See chapter 4.

Provide ongoing training. Give ongoing training to your team, bring in experts, and send them to seminars to get certifications that raise their capacity as employees. Help your team pursue continuous learning. This will make them stronger teammates and keep their minds engaged in their work.

Develop each team member. Your team members need to know where they stand. A great framework for this is the performance review, but it's most helpful when it's used as an ongoing development tool throughout the year. You outline ways for them to grow in fulfilling their job description at the beginning of the year, check on their progress throughout the year, and let them know where they stand each time you revisit it. This becomes an objective method to measuring whether your employee is meeting, exceeding, or falling short of your expectations. Great employees are always looking to move to the next level in their profession, and this helps them see their path to reach that next level. Do they need to acquire a new technical skill, be a better team player, or make more efficient use of time or materials?

Foster real relationships between team members. Facilitate discussions amongst them about what they're learning. Help them to appreciate each other's personalities and strengths, which should improve their teamwork. Get them together for informal outings that you fund. Have fun together as we advise in chapter 14. Such bonding can bring outsized improvements in team chemistry.

Get your team to brainstorm new ideas. Foster an environment where employees are at ease to share their ideas. Your best innovations may come from these men and women who work daily with your products and customers. Invite their ideas through one-on-one interaction, staff meetings, and even suggestion boxes. Regularly ask: "How can we improve?" Not only will this drive innovation, but having a voice will increase employee engagement.

Celebrate team victories. See chapter 14 for our advice on rewarding individual achievement, but also consider ways to reward the entire team when they come together to achieve something superb. Even buying your team lunch, coffee, or a snack to celebrate a small victory can motivate employees and build team loyalty.

Build a strong leadership team. Bring key people from each part of the company that you want to develop as leaders. Invest in them at regular leadership team meetings where they help to solve companywide problems and work out the inevitable communication issues, which is what the Tree Work Now leadership team spends the most time on. Most of these people problems center on "fear of conflict, lack of focus, lack of discipline, lack of commitment, and personal ego" (Wickman p.136). How important is a cohesive leadership team? "As goes the leadership team, so goes the company". In fact, Patrick Lencioni makes a healthy leadership team his first requirement for building a world class organization (Wickman p.17).

Disagree and commit. My wrestling team would always spar furiously with each other, then stand utterly united against an opposing team. Amazon CEO Jeff Bezos suggests asking your leadership team to adopt this practice. Encourage open debate, but once a consensus has been reached, dissenters agree to support the team decision. "You're all in. No sabotaging the project – directly or indirectly. By trusting your team's gut, you give them room to experiment and grow – and your people gain confidence." This means at times not using your veto power. I disagreed with my leadership team on how to administer our winter savings program, but decided that empowering them was more important that following my better judgment. It would be different if it was a bigger decision or one that would have compromised our core values.

Cross-train employees. This has two valuable benefits. For one, it raises the capacity of your team, making it easier to fill a gap internally when you lose a key employee. It also builds an understanding of the challenges other teammates face daily in their jobs. There's nothing like walking a mile in someone else's shoes to appreciate their perspective. That shared experience creates empathy that destroys the us vs. them mentality.

Case Study

I (Evan) have seen teams really come together by discovering their personality types (Myers-Briggs) or personal strengths (StrengthsFinder). They benefited from the individual self-awareness and also finally saw why team members act in certain ways. They appreciated each other more and learned how to better lean on each other and work together without making each other crazy. This can resolve underlying tensions and lead to more productive teamwork. But I believe the best team bonding comes through overcoming obstacles and achieving something big together. I've experienced this in leading a team, whether it's putting on conferences and mission trips or writing a book together. Another avenue is an outdoor adventure in which you push your athletic limits and face difficult weather, leaning on each other as a team. Be careful – this can backfire! Intensive experiences like this expose the weaknesses of your own leadership. Taking a team on the Appalachian Trail, including long days in the rain with an out-of-shape team lugging heavy backpacks up-up-up the mountain highlighted my tendency to push people beyond their limits. I may have learned the most. The humility was good for me and the adversity made some memories that brought our team together – in spite of me!

Leading Self, Employees, Systems

SELF – Keep a close pulse on team dynamics, dealing with small problems before they grow and ruin the positive teamwork you've nurtured. Beware of only focusing on results without nurturing the people and conditions that will produce them.

EMPLOYEES – Treat them as humans (chapter 14). Stay in touch with them. Be responsive to their concerns and ideas. See their potential. Develop them and challenge them so they have opportunities to make satisfying contributions to the team.

SYSTEMS – Discuss self-discovery tools to help team members understand themselves and each other better. Use performance reviews and ongoing training to develop your team.

NOW WHAT?

Summary

Individuals going in different directions cannot achieve team goals. Your goals can only be achieved when you make the mission clear and gather the team around shared goals that align with values you enforce. Set clear expectations and use performance reviews and ongoing training to spur development of your team members. Encourage relationships and idea generation amongst them in a fun, but high-performance atmosphere. Reward and celebrate team victories.

Application Questions

1. Which skills and behaviors should be on your hiring checklist?
2. Who do you need to terminate or reassign to improve team effectiveness?
3. How can you raise the standard of what is expected of your team and hold them to it?

4. How will you better model what you expect from your team?

5. How will you discover the strengths of your team members and actively develop them?

6. What types of training will you use in the coming year to help your team learn and grow?

7. Will you conduct annual performance reviews? How often will you revisit them to spur development throughout the year?

8. How will you get your team to generate ideas to improve the company?

9. What fun activities will you schedule to nurture relationships between team members?

10. How will you recognize and reward team accomplishments?

Recommended Reading

The Five Dysfunctions of a Team, by Patrick Lencioni

Harvard Business Review on Building Better Teams, by Bob Frisch

Make it Happen!

What ideas has this chapter stirred in me?

What new light does this chapter shine on my leadership and my business?

What changes do I plan to make?

My actions to *Make it Happen!*	Completion dates	
	Proposed	Actual

Circle the appropriate action for each topic:

5. Employees

13. Hire & Delegate to Leaders - *Have I appointed and empowered leaders over sales, office, and production?*

        Maintain   Fine-Tune   Overhaul

14. Engage Employees - *Have I built a positive company culture so that employees care about the company and their work?*

        Maintain   Fine-Tune   Overhaul

15. Build Teamwork - *Am I developing team members and the team as a whole, helping them work together to achieve clear goals that align with our values?*

        Maintain   Fine-Tune   Overhaul

MY #1 FOCUS: _____

6. Finance

Steadily build wealth by being: vigilant in managing cash, diligent in saving, frugal with spending, strategic in negotiating, cautious with borrowing, and careful in protecting your business.

Chapter 16 | Achieve Positive Cash Flow

By Evan Keller

WHAT?

Definition

Positive cash flow starts with understanding the cash flow cycle: Sales ➔ Collections ➔ Cash ➔ Payments to Suppliers & Employees ➔ Sales. Effective cash flow management speeds the movement of cash through the cash flow cycle, making it available to operate and grow the business. A business reaches positive cash flow when it produces efficiently and generates sufficient high-margin sales.

Expert Quote

"Sales are nice. Profits are nicer. But you live or die on cash flow." (Norm Brodsky, as quoted in <u>Small Giants</u>, p.156)

Assessment Questions

1. How have you used the pressure of keeping cash flowing to spur efficiency and innovation?
2. How long has it been since your last cash flow crisis?
3. How long could your business operate on your current cash reserves?

WHY?

Benefits

Survival. In the limited context of business survival, we agree with Pehr Gyllenhammar (former CEO of Volvo) that "cash is king." You need cash to operate. If you run out of cash, you can't do business. Without paid employees and purchased supplies, there will be no future products to sell. If cash flow is interrupted for too long, you are finished! You're officially bankrupt when your short-term liabilities exceed your short-term assets.

Relief. A huge sigh of relief comes when your business finally becomes viable, that is, "the point at which the company can sustain itself on its own internally generated cash flow" (Norm Brodsky, Street Smarts, p.x).

Options. More funds can be saved, invested, and donated when cash flow is positive. You can finally be paid for your years of hard work! You can also focus more energy and creativity on long-term growth.

Debt Reduction. Focus can shift from making payroll to managing your long-term debt load. Shorter terms and bigger down payments on capital loans allow you to pay off your equipment and property sooner, pay less interest, and reduce overall debt load.

Self-determination. Viable businesses are less dependent on lenders and can self-fund some of their growth.

Barriers

External causes of cash flow crises: increasing raw material costs, increasing taxes, more competitors, low-pricecompetitors, price-shopping consumers, declining demand, theft, fire, storms, lack of access to capital, customers who don't pay, and political and economic conditions.

Internal causes of cash flow crises: wasted time and materials, prices too low, salaries too high, loans to family or friends in need, inefficient collection and credit policies and practices, not saving money for the slow season, and growing too fast.

Underlying Values

Responsibility. Although external causes are real, they've not made it impossible to function in your market. Instead of using things you cannot change as an excuse for doing nothing, focus on the internal causes of your cash flow crises – and fix them before it's too late. Here is a negative example to avoid: "A sluggard says, 'There's a lion in the road, a fierce lion roaming the streets!'" – Proverbs 26:13

Patience and emotional resilience. Both are necessary to weather the lean early years. The constant battle to make payroll can either stress you to the breaking point or increase your toughness. – Genesis 29:20-28

Frugality. "Cash is hard to get and easy to spend. Make it before you spend it" (Norm Brodsky, Street Smart, p.x). Exercise the steady discipline of avoiding purchases that don't really benefit your business. And negotiate good deals on the purchases you *do* make (chapter 19).

HOW?

Steps to Implement

When in a cash flow crisis, take these *short-term* steps to accelerate the cash flow cycle:

1. Ask for payment from customers who are late, starting with the most recent.

2. Explain the situation to your suppliers and ask for extended payment terms. To maintain trust, it's better to pay part of what you owe *on time* rather than to pay it all late.

3. Sell unneeded assets.

4. Discount products that are not selling.

5. Reduce your own salary.

6. Pay subcontractors after you are paid on their projects, if it accords with your agreement with them.

Whereas swiftly taking the above steps can get cash flowing again for the moment, they won't resolve the underlying causes. To move from surviving to thriving, you'll need to make deeper systemic changes over time, including implementing the following *long-term* systems to prevent cash flow crises from happening again:

Make sales at sufficient margins and volume. Sell less of your low margin products and more of your high margin products or introduce new ones. Know your break-even point for each product line and make sure you have healthy margins to cover costs and provide profit. Train your salesforce to communicate the value your company offers and show them how to courageously ask for the prices you need (chapter 11). Whenever possible, raise your prices slowly over time, showing clients how you are providing additional value. Customers understand that costs go up incrementally as do their incomes. Know the volume of sales needed to have a healthy debt-service ratio and cover your fixed costs. Beware of only focusing on increasing revenue as entrepreneurs often underestimate the additional cost of creating new revenue. "If you just track sales, you can get into serious trouble. Sales don't make a company successful. Profits and cash flow do. A lot of companies land in bankruptcy court because their owners focus so much on driving sales that profit and cash become an afterthought" (Norm Brodsky <u>Street Smarts</u> p.79).

Reduce production costs by tracking expenses and eliminating waste. By looking monthly at your top five expenses (and any other expense categories known to be waste-prone) on your profit & loss statement, you'll come to know when they are unusually high, prompting you to find out why and fix it. Since most of your expenses will grow with your business, it is more important to track their ratio to overall revenue rather than the actual dollar amount. For example, a bakery's flour costs will grow as it produces more bread, but if its ratio to overall revenue (cost of flour in a month divided by that month's total bread sales) goes up significantly compared to other months, it alerts the baker that some of the flour is being wasted or her employees are making her loaves too large or too many loaves are going bad before they can be sold. See chapter 18.

Develop an efficient inventory management system, utilizing software for your industry if available. By regularly tracking sales of each item, begin "just in time" ordering of materials and inventory, so you rarely have too little or too much of each item – keeping your clients happy without tying up too much capital. Smaller, more frequent orders will preserve cash flow, although you may want to make larger orders when volume discounts are available or when you have reason to believe that prices will soon rise dramatically. See chapter 10.

Develop a system to quickly collect payments from clients. Require immediate cash payments whenever possible. Set short timeframes between the sale, delivering the invoice, and collecting the payment. Communicate your expectations to customers and stop selling to those who consistently pay late. You may want to offer an incentive to those who pay quickly. Keep an up-to-date accounts receivable aging spreadsheet, showing which accounts are 30, 60, and 90+ days behind in paying you, with appropriate collections actions being taken at each stage.

Develop a system to save money, building cash reserves to prevent future cash crises and even purchase new equipment.

When cash flow is tight, it seems impossible to save any money at all. But even if it's a very small amount, establishing this habit is an important character-building discipline. Set a weekly savings target that is challenging, but achievable with determination and effort. This builds an internal safety net to bail yourself out of cash flow crises. See more in the next chapter (17).

Case Study

I started Tree Work Now in 2005 with a 1979 borrowed truck and two borrowed chainsaws. On the first job, the truck got stuck and the saws both broke. We've always operated without injections of capital from owners or outside investors. Local community banks wrote small equipment loans, growing larger with proven payment history, solid growth, and healthy debt-service ratio. I began paying myself a minimal regular salary in year four. We've always been able to pay our bills on time, but there was never much left over – getting easier by the year. Even in year eight there were a couple of weeks when we barely made payroll. After years of focus on cutting costs and increasing the margin and volume of our sales, we finally had breathing room in year nine. What a feeling!

Leading Self, Employees, Systems

SELF – Controlling costs and setting money aside illustrate a key entrepreneurial discipline: making sacrifices *now* to build value for the *future*. You've likely seen many new business owners driving shiny new vehicles. They got things backwards! In year 11, I was driving an 11-year-old truck. Then after I updated the fleet of revenue-generating heavy equipment, it was finally the right time to buy my first new truck. If you struggle to do this consistently, be sure to ask a mentor or friend to keep you accountable. Reflect regularly on the vision of your company to remind yourself why you've chosen this difficult path.

EMPLOYEES – Ensure accounts receivable staff are following your system or collecting promptly, ensure salespeople are getting good margins and sufficient volume, instill a culture of frugality and efficiency and reward those who exemplify it. Above all, never be late in paying them. This is a sacred trust between you. Make this number one obligation to them the top priority use of your cash. If you breech this trust even once, low employee morale may plague your business and your best employees may look for a more dependable employer. "Do not make your hired workers wait until the next day to receive their pay" (Leviticus 19:13). If you treat your employees right, they will be slightly less likely to steal from you, abuse your equipment and facilities, or waste time and materials.

SYSTEMS – In addition to the systems suggested above, you may need a customer credit policy in which customers are required to prove their creditworthiness. "When you deliver a product or a service before getting paid, you're making a loan to the customer, and you should treat it accordingly. That means determining whether customers are creditworthy" (Norm Brodsky <u>Street Smarts</u> p.xi).

NOW WHAT?

Summary

While it's tempting to blame external causes for your cash flow crises, entrepreneurs must focus on the internal causes they *can* influence. While quick fixes can provide temporary relief, long-term viability requires increasing margins, controlling costs, managing inventory, collecting quickly, and building savings. This milestone requires discipline and patience to reach.

Application Questions

1. What are the external and internal causes of your cash flow crises?
2. Which of the above short-term fixes should you do now?
3. Which of the above long-term systems should you build, and in what order?

4. What current or future products or services will provide you the best margins?

5. Do you need to raise your prices to cover costs and provide a sufficient profit margin?

6. What are your largest and most waste-prone expense categories?

7. How can you improve your inventory management system?

8. Do you regularly check the state of your receivables and is your average collection time appropriate?

9. What should your current savings goals be – weekly and cumulative?

Recommended Reading

Street Smarts by Norm Brodsky and Bo Burlingham

Make it Happen!

What ideas has this chapter stirred in me?

What new light does this chapter shine on my leadership and my business?

What changes do I plan to make?

My actions to *Make it Happen!*	Completion dates	
	Proposed	Actual

Chapter 17 | Save Money Diligently

By Jennifer Pettie & Evan Keller

WHAT?

Definition

"Retained earnings" are monies you set aside from internally generated cash flow. Even if it seems impossible at present, start saving even a very small amount every week. Put it in a separate account, working towards graduated goals until you eventually have three months of working capital and can even buy equipment from your retained earnings. A regular savings plan is an important part of achieving positive cash flow.

Expert Quote

"The habit of saving is itself an education; it fosters every virtue, teaches self-denial, cultivates the sense of order, trains to forethought, and so broadens the mind." –T.T. Munger http://www.forbes.com/sites/robertberger/2014/04/30/top-100-money-quotes-of-all-time/, quote # 51.

Assessment Questions

1. Do you have a business savings account and how often do you deposit to it?
2. If you're not currently saving, do you see any benefit of saving even 1% of your revenue per week?
3. Do you have trouble making payroll?
4. What safety nets do you have in place to recover from a cash flow crisis?

WHY?

Benefits

Peace of mind. Not worrying about making payroll reduces stress and frees up your mind and energy for creative ideas to grow your business.

Expanded options. Liquidity increases the agility of your business. You can accept a large order and be able to buy the raw materials you'll need. You can launch a new product or make a new hire. Or when an excellent deal comes along, you won't miss the opportunity while waiting for a loan.

Satisfaction. Look at savings as the business paying itself for all its hard work. If every dollar that comes in goes right out the back door, it makes you ask "Is this worth all the trouble?" But steadily growing some retained earnings gives you a sense of progress.

Access to capital. More liquidity will make your balance sheet healthier. Lenders will see that you have the ability to pay back their loans.

Barriers

Scarcity of funds. No matter how much is in your operating account, your business will tend to spend it all. See the previous chapter (18) on cash flow.

Scarcity of attention. "Scarcity of attention prevents us from seeing what's really important. The psychology of scarcity engrosses us in only our present needs" (Sendhil Mullainathan, "Why is Saving Money So Hard? (Time Magazine, http://time.com/money/671/why-is-saving-money-so-hard/).

Scarcity mindset. Because you're used to just scraping by each week, you may assume it's impossible for you to save anything. This mental block is a more formidable barrier than actually finding funds to save.

Underlying Values

Patience. Act now for long-term results. – Proverbs 21:5

Hope. You won't save unless you believe you can make a positive impact on your future. – Proverbs 13:12

Discipline. Saving requires focused attention over a long period of time. – Proverbs 30:25

Frugality. An older member of your family could likely give great advice on this. Watching your pennies will allow you to be generous where it's important – see chapter 24.

HOW?

Steps to Implement

Start now. Even if cash flow is tight and your deposits are tiny, saving is a character-building discipline.

Control spending closely. This creates a margin for savings. This includes making a budget. See the next chapter (18) for details. If you don't tell your money where to go, you will wonder where it went.

Open a separate account for savings. Obviously, if it's in the same pool of funds as your operating account, it will get spent on regular expenses. A separate account makes it harder to spend and requires an intentional decision to use it to fund an opportunity or bail out a cash flow crisis.

Decide on a minimum weekly deposit. Even if it's very small, pay the business first. The simplest way to build savings is to never give yourself the chance to spend the money in the first place. When cash flow is strong, make additional savings deposits above and beyond your minimum weekly goal. As able, continue raising your weekly deposit amount.

Automate your savings. Set up an automatic weekly withdrawal from checking into your savings account if your bank has this option. This forces you to be disciplined.

Set graduated cumulative goals. Aim first to accumulate one pay period's worth of payroll. This will give you a little peace of mind, knowing that you have the margin to at least fulfil your most important commitment. Then accumulate one month's operating costs, then two, then three. Corporate business experts suggest having six months of operating capital on hand, but have they ever run a small business?

Save for your slow season. If your business has strong seasonal fluctuations, then you need to dramatically boost your savings amount during your busy season. In the slow season, try to hold out as long as possible from making withdrawals.

Save for equipment purchases. After you gain some breathing room with general savings, you may want to establish a separate account for future equipment purchases. Even if this practice does not enable you to buy equipment with 100% cash, it will help you to make larger than usual down payments.

Withdraw as needed. Make this a last resort, and don't let it discourage you. Rather, be thankful that you were able to save to make the crisis more manageable.

Establish a timeframe for your goals. A great motivational tool is to give yourself ambitious, yet achievable deadlines for attaining your goals.

Take the long view. You are used to getting things done – producing results. But saving months of operating capital is one of the *slowest* of all business goals to accomplish. Don't lose heart. It *is* possible.

Case Study

Tree Work Now Inc is in a sharply seasonal industry. Christmas trees are the only trees people spend money on in the winter! They suddenly remember their living trees when spring hits – while planting flowers and hearing about impending hurricane. Managing for three months of slow sales is a major undertaking, making saving money regularly even more crucial. An added challenge is that employees want a bonus at Christmas time! We make automatic investments for as much of the year as possible, and try to spend as little of that as possible in the winter. This has allowed us to fund a winter savings program for our employees. We match all funds they direct-deposit from their pay into their own savings accounts – up to $2,000/person (distributed during the slowest month of our year). This allows us to give a Christmas bonus while also encouraging good financial habits. Even though we're cash flow positive, we are far from our goal of having six months of operating capital in savings and investments. Patience.

Leading Self, Employees, Systems

SELF – Once you overcome the formidable mental barrier to believing you can actually build up some savings, getting going is super simple. After setting up your savings account, it only takes small doses of attention to adjust your deposit amounts up and down (if necessary) as you go.

EMPLOYEES – Explain the connection between the company's liquidity and their own livelihoods. Consider employee incentives for helping you reach the company's savings goals, and a matching program for their personal savings.

SYSTEMS – Good savings systems include an automatic savings plan into a separate account, a plan to manage seasonal cash fluctuations, and a timeframe to reach savings goals. See the next chapter (18) for financial systems such as budgeting and cash flow forecasting.

NOW WHAT?

Summary

Once you overcome the mental barriers and accept that it will be a long fight, your likelihood of successfully saving increases dramatically. The biggest key is to just get started right away. Taking the simple steps of establishing separate accounts, regular automatic deposits, and graduated goals will get you on your way to saving up for future operating expenses, equipment, and seasonal fluctuations. Adjust along the way and persevere as you move slowly toward your goals.

Application Questions

1. How will you overcome the scarcity mindset? Can you think of a fellow entrepreneur brimming with positivity and determination who can encourage you towards your savings goals?
2. How will you nurture the underlying values of hope, discipline, frugality, and patience?
3. How much will you deposit into savings each week?
4. Will you set it up to transfer automatically?
5. What is your initial cumulative savings goal and when do you hope to reach it? What will you shoot for next?
6. Are you ready to begin saving for equipment purchases?
7. What is your plan to save for seasonal cash flow fluctuations?

Recommended Reading

Entreleadership - Dave Ramsey

Thou Shall Prosper – Rabbi Daniel Lapin

Make it Happen!

What ideas has this chapter stirred in me?

What new light does this chapter shine on my leadership and my business?

What changes do I plan to make?

My actions to *Make it Happen!*	Completion dates	
	Proposed	Actual

Chapter 18 | Control Spending Closely

By Evan Keller

Definition

Knowing your financial position and tracking your expenses period-to-period are important to leading your business well. Controlling and tracking spending provides necessary accountability for your team.

Expert Quote

"You have to know enough accounting to figure out which numbers are most important in your particular business, and then you should develop the habit of watching them like a hawk" (Norm Brodsky, Street Smarts, p.ix).

Assessment Questions

1. How would you rate the financial health of your business? What specific numbers do you base that on?
2. Is your use of financials an afterthought or do you read them to make better decisions?
3. Do you know your biggest sources of waste?
4. Do you monitor all of your employees' purchases?

WHY?

Benefits

Clarity. Knowing your financial health makes decisions a lot easier. It increases your confidence to lead your company forward.

Foresight. Seeing trends in your numbers can help you make changes to avert financial disaster.

Savings. Waste is eliminated when you ensure all purchases are authorized, and when you find ways to do more with less.

Barriers

Complexity. Numbers scare people, and reading financial statements takes time and effort.

Personality. Many entrepreneurs are big picture visionaries who can't be bothered with the details.

Busyness. Everything else seems more urgent, so tedious tasks of tracking spending and analyzing financials can get pushed aside.

Underlying Values

Attention. Know when your payments will come in and where every expense is going. – Proverbs 27:23

Efficiency. Without it, you can't provide value to your customers and generate a profit at the same time.

Accountability. Wise stewardship of money is essential for financial health and team trust. – Like 16:1-10

HOW?

Steps to Implement

Use financials to track and improve efficiencies:

Produce monthly financial statements. Some will need them to make decisions even more often. Others will be most helped by analyzing longer trends over a three month period. Mid-year (June 30) and year-end (December 31) statements deserve an even closer look. Use software, such as QuickBooks, to produce their financial statements. As long as all business transactions for a period have been properly inputted, you can instantly produce accurate financial statements with such software.

Understand the difference between a balance sheet and a profit and loss (income) statement. A balance sheet is a snapshot in time of your company's financial health. Like an x-ray, it shows how things look today, but includes the factors that led up to today just as smoking in the past contributes to today's lung condition. Whereas a balance sheet reflects a moment in time, a profit and loss statement shows what's come in and out over a particular period, such as a month, quarter, or year. It allows you to track trends in expense categories, as well as important sums such as total revenue, cost of goods sold, gross and net profit.

Correctly categorize fixed versus variable costs. Fixed costs are payments you must make whether or not you make any sales in a particular period - such as utilities. Variable costs increase as your sales and production increase – such as raw materials. These two types of costs are listed in separate categories on your profit and loss statement: fixed costs under "expenses" and variable costs under "cost of goods sold." If you miscategorize your costs, then your financial statements will not be accurate, and they will be less helpful in making good decisions. You will know better than your accountant whether an expense category varies proportionately with production, so discuss whether his/her assumptions fit your business. The official definition reads: "Fixed costs are expenses that do not vary with sales volume, such as rent and administrative salaries. These expenses must be paid regardless of sales and are often referred to as overhead costs. Variable costs fluctuate directly with sales volume, such as purchasing inventory, shipping, and manufacturing a product" (https://www.sba.gov/content/breakeven-analysis).

Use your profit and loss statement to track your top five expense categories period-to-period. For many small businesses, month-to-month comparisons will be the most meaningful. Since many businesses have predictable seasonal fluctuations in sales, comparing a month to the same month last year and the year before yield a reliable measure of growth. (You could also compare to previous months, average of the last three months, and year-to-date average.) You should scan all expense categories for anything unusual, but then track the ones that are most important. This should include your top five categories, but also any category that is especially prone to waste. In addition to tracking the raw numbers, use ratios to see if the expenses are growing or shrinking in proportion to overall revenue. Calculate this percentage like this: expense category total / revenue total. (This ratio can also be helpful: expense category total / total of all expenses.) Once you have the period-to-period comparisons in front of you, it's time to look for trends and ask *why*. Did you spend more than usual on fuel last month because (1) fuel prices went up, (2) you made more deliveries than usual, (3) a new driver does not know the best routes, (4) or an employee is fueling up his/her personal vehicle?

It's not enough to produce and know your numbers, you've got to *use* them to discern what's going on in your business and make the necessary improvements.

Identify your single most important ratio. Which single number gives you the best insight as to how efficiently your business is producing? It will vary from business to business.

Know your "current ratio." This liquidity ratio measures your ability to meet your short-term debt obligations. Calculate by dividing current assets by current liabilities (from your balance sheet). A ratio higher than 1.25 is healthy. You may be in trouble if under 1.0.

Know your EBITDA. Say what?! EBITDA is "Earnings Before Interest, Tax, Depreciation and Amortization. According to investinganswers.com, it "is a measure of a company's operating performance. Essentially, it's a way to evaluate a company's performance without having to factor in financing decisions, accounting decisions or tax environments.

EBITDA is calculated by adding back the non-cash expenses of depreciation and amortization to a firm's operating income.

Earnings Before Interest, Taxes, Depreciation, and Amortization

$$\left.\begin{array}{l}\text{Net Income} \\ + \text{ Interest Expense} \\ + \text{ Taxes} \\ + \text{ Depreciation} \\ + \text{ Amortization}\end{array}\right] = \text{EBITDA}$$

EBIDTA allows you to focus on the outcome of operating decisions while excluding the impacts of non-operating decisions like interest expenses (a financing decision), tax rates (a governmental decision), or large non-cash items like depreciation and amortization (an accounting decision).

By minimizing the non-operating effects that are unique to each company, EBITDA allows investors to focus on operating profitability as a singular measure of performance" (http://www.investinganswers.com/financial-dictionary/financial-statement-analysis/earnings-interest-tax-depreciation-and-amortizatio).

Know your gross margin. While many entrepreneurs obsess over driving sales, they forget to be diligent about the *quality* of those sales. That can be measured by gross margin – that is, "the percentage of your money left over after accounting for the direct cost of whatever it is that you're selling. (Gross profit is sales minus cost of goods sold. Divide that by sales to figure gross margin.) I believe gross margin is one of the most important numbers, if not *the* most important number, in any business" (Norm Brodsky, Street Smarts, p.x). Now if you have multiple product lines, you'll want to find out which of them have higher gross margins, so you can focus on selling more of them, and possibly phasing out those with the lowest gross margins. To do so, you'll need to track these separately for each product line: sales, cost of goods sold, gross profit, and gross margin. If you find yourself with lots of low-margin sales, Brodsky says you have four options to correct it: "raise your prices, reduce your manufacturing costs, say no to low-margin business, or find other products you can sell at higher margins" (p.76).

Know your break-even point. By looking at all your costs, you can see whether your pricing takes into account all your production, distribution, and marketing costs, while allowing for a healthy profit margin.

$$\text{Breakeven Point} = \frac{\text{Fixed Costs}}{\text{Price Per Unit} - \text{Variable Cost Per Unit}}$$

Use a "dashboard" for a quick view of numbers you're tracking. Once you've identified what you want to track, use a dashboard program to get real-time information you'd like to see daily (or at least weekly). These programs extract data from QuickBooks and automatically populate the totals and ratios that are most important to you now. This quick-scan feature increases the likelihood that you'll use your financials.

Learn from your accountant. Your accountant may just want to get your taxes done and be done with you. Don't be content with that. Get him or her to educate you on reading financials. The top ten questions to ask your accountant are:

1. How would you assess the overall financial health of my business? Which numbers on these financials tell you that?
2. What is my break-even point and where do I stand in relation to it?
3. Do you think I would qualify for a loan and afford to pay it back?

4. What trends do you see in my numbers and what do you they mean?
5. What financial ratios do you think are most important for my business (gross margin, current ratio, debt-equity ratio, etc.)?
6. How do my expenses compare to other businesses my size?
7. Where do you suspect I could reduce waste?
8. How often do you suggest I analyze my financials?
9. What tax strategy do you recommend this year?
10. Would it be more tax-advantageous to buy equipment this year or next?

Make industry comparisons. Try to find out how your expenses compare to averages for a business your size and type in your area. Your industry's trade association or fee-based companies may be able to provide this information.

Compare "actuals" to budgets. "One of the most important financial management exercises is the creation and use of a budget – the examination of all your expenses and estimation of what they will be next year. This will automatically get you thinking of the drivers behind each expense. And don't worry, your estimates will nearly always be off-target, but if you understand *why* a line item is going considerably over budget, you'll know what to fix and how" (Joe Worth, Entrepreneur Magazine, October 2012, p.90). A budget is merely a projected profit and loss statement for next year. Dave Ramsey likens using a budget to looking through the windshield at what's coming ahead and using a profit and loss statement to looking at your rear-view mirror to see what's already transpired. Obviously, you need both. Budgeting only effectively tells your money where to go if you use it throughout the year (EntreLeadership p.193).

Establish and monitor tight financial controls:

Scan your bank and credit card statements each month. "Until you know where all your money is going, your business isn't on sound footing" (Joe Worth, Entrepreneur Magazine, August 2013, p.76). Look at each check and each credit card purchase for anything that may not be a true business expense. Circle it and ask the employee who made the purchase about it. Don't make it confrontational, but rather explain that this is a standard procedure for a well-run business. It can deepen trust with those who are trustworthy while exposing those who are not. The two employees we've caught using their credit card for personal purchases were making very small purchases they thought we wouldn't notice. So, don't just look at the big numbers.

Establish checks and balances. There should be more than one set of eyes on every financial process done by your office staff. For example, if one person makes the deposits (especially if cash is involved), a different person should input them into QuickBooks. Accountant Jennifer Pettie expounds on this: "separation of duties is key to handling money and doing bookkeeping. This reduces the chances for erroneous and inappropriate actions. Simply stated, the approval function, the accounting/reconciling function, and the cash custody responsibilities should be separated amongst employees. When these job duties cannot be separated, close monitoring by supervisors is required. Separation of duties provides checks and balances against fraud because it requires cooperate with another person to perpetrate a fraudulent act."

These are a few examples of separation of duties:

- The person who requests the purchase of goods or services should not be the person who approves the purchase.

- The person who approves the purchase of goods or services should not be the person who reconciles the monthly financial reports.

- The person who approves the purchase of goods or services should not be able to obtain custody of checks.

- The person who maintains and reconciles the accounting records should not be able to obtain custody of checks.

- The person who receives customer payments and prepares a listing of them should not be the person who makes the deposit and maintains the accounts receivable records.

Set limits on what employees can purchase without your authorization. Obviously, you'll want to negotiate the major purchases, such as equipment, insurance, and property – see the next chapter for negotiation strategies. Make clear to those few with check-writing privileges what they are authorized to do on their own. Set appropriate limits on all credit cards, and issue a credit card usage policy that employees sign. Disable the cash back feature of your credit cards and be aware that debit cards don't have the same fraud protection as credit cards.

Hire the right people. As your company grows and finances become more complex, you may need to hire a controller or chief financial officer. But most small businesses rely on a bookkeeper (in-house or out-sourced) along with their accountant, who double-checks the bookkeeper's work and oversees equipment depreciation and tax strategy.

Case Study

It is important for both cash flow and overall financial health to identify the one ratio which is the most reliable indicator of its profitability. Then you can track it and work to improve it. For example, since my company is a service business and payroll is our largest expense by far, we track that ratio (total employee wages for the month divided by that month's total sales) every month. Depending on the time of year, and how well our salespeople and crews are doing, our payroll ratio fluctuates between 32 and 45% of revenue. Our target is 33%, and even when not realistic to meet it, we want to be as close as possible, not fluctuating so widely. If our salespeople get the right prices for our jobs and our crews complete them in an efficient manner, we'll reduce that ratio and improve our overall profitability.

Leading Self, Employees, Systems

SELF – While bookkeepers and accountants are helpful, *you've* got to know your numbers and use them to make good decisions.

EMPLOYEES – Every employee contributes in some way to costs, so nurture a culture of frugality. If they're not happy with their jobs, they may intentionally waste or even steal.

SYSTEMS – Checks and balances, accountability for purchases on bank and credit card statements, and tracking ratios period-to-period are all helpful processes.

NOW WHAT?

Summary

Numbers run a business; if you don't know your numbers, you're flying blind (Norm Brodsky). Using financials to track expenses can move you from operating on instinct and guesswork to making decisions from reliable information. Likewise, tracking checks and credit card purchases will keep your employees honest and remind them that controlling costs is important.

Application Questions

1. How can you improve accountability for purchases?
2. How can you improve your system of checks and balances?
3. Which of the 'top ten questions for your accountant' will you use in your next meeting?
4. Which expense categories and ratios will you begin tracking?

5. Where do you think you can eliminate waste this year?

6. Will you create a budget?

7. What numbers will you track for tax purposes?

8. How often will you analyze your financials?

9. Will you use a financial dashboard for quick reference?

Recommended Reading

Street Smarts by Norm Brodsky and Bo Burlingham

Make it Happen!

What ideas has this chapter stirred in me?

What new light does this chapter shine on my leadership and my business?

What changes do I plan to make?

My actions to *Make it Happen!*	Completion dates	
	Proposed	Actual

Chapter 19 | Negotiate Good Deals

By Evan Keller

WHAT?

Definition

Getting great value on all your major expenses and sales is vital to the financial health and longevity of your business. Much of what you do in business involves negotiating, whether it's buying, selling, leasing, bartering or contracting with: employees or subcontractors, partners or investors, suppliers or customers, landlords or tenants.

Expert Quote

"Negotiate first about a secondary matter, understanding that – at the end of the process – you'll probably let the other party get most of what it wants on the issue in question. Your concession on the first negotiating point will give you additional bargaining power when you bring your number one issue to the table" (Norm Brodsky <u>Street Smarts</u> p.93).

Assessment Questions

1. What is the best deal you've gotten? What made it so great?

2. What is the worst business deal you've made and what have you learned from it?

3. How would you rate your negotiation skills?

WHY?

Benefits

Efficiency. Good businesses create value by doing more with less, providing unique solutions at prices that customers are willing to pay. All of this is undercut if you don't negotiate good deals on your inputs.

Viability. Getting good value for your money is important to achieving positive cash flow.

Longevity. If you feel guilty for being a tough negotiator, remind yourself that being efficient today will help your business be around to provide jobs and serve customers in the future.

Barriers

Assumptions. You may think you know what the other party wants, but you don't truly know until you listen well.

Intimidation. Do not give in to pressure or fear. As powerful as the other party may be, they also seem to want what you have. Don't do a deal that doesn't make sense for you.

Impatience. Know when to await their next move and don't short-cut your research. Being over-eager may land you a bad deal.

Underlying Values

Fairness. Treat people as humans with immeasurable intrinsic value, rather than just using them to get what you want. – Proverbs 11:1, 3

Integrity. Keep your promises and be willing to lose money to make things right on a deal you or your employees messed up. – James 5:12

Slow to speak. "If one gives an answer before he hears, it is his folly and shame." – Proverbs 18:13

Value for customers. If you get good deals on your raw materials and equipment, you can pass on that value to your customers while still making a profit.

Courage. Know when to hold your ground.

Discernment. Know when to give ground to land a deal you really want. – Ecclesiastes 3:1

HOW?

Steps to Implement

Be aware of seasonal shifts in the market. Is what your buying or selling in higher demand during certain parts of the year? I had to accept a lower price when I sold a travel trailer in January, four months before camping season began. Do you need to proceed now or can you wait until a more optimal time to find what you want at the right price?

Know what you're buying. Do the necessary research to understand the product or service you're considering. This is especially true with complex services such as insurance, financing, and payroll services. The casual buyer won't get a good deal because they don't even know what terms to ask for. Read the fine print of what they're offering as well as researching the industry. The best way to find out what terms to negotiate is to ask multiple suppliers: "How is your product different from what your competitors offer?" Use a spreadsheet to compare companies' offerings to narrow it down to three you want to explore further.

Identify your needs and prioritize them. Know exactly what you want out of the deal and which of those wants are must-haves. Write them down to help clarify them to yourself.

Keep your top priorities to yourself. Do your homework to find out if suppliers can meet your needs without spelling out what's most important to you. Make your top priority one of the many terms of the deal, without drawing too much attention to it. If you tell them they're the only one who has what you want, you'll have no bargaining power.

Negotiate with more than one supplier, going to your preferred negotiating partner last. Let the other parties know you're getting several quotes. They may sharpen their pencil to win your business. Negotiate the best possible deal with your second best supplier, then use that to leverage the deal you want with your preferred supplier. Use one deal to leverage another, then you can revisit the second best supplier if your preferred deal falls through.

Maintain two suppliers for all your major expenses. In his INC Magazine column, Norm Brodsky recommends that you always keep a primary supplier, and a second one to keep the first one honest. If the first raises their prices, lowers their quality, has poor service, or goes out of business, you have someone else who can quickly fill the void.

Meet face-to-face, but only after you've already negotiated into your range of possibility. Meeting in person shows a level of commitment you don't want to make until they've demonstrated that they're serious enough to move in your direction. But you need to meet face-to-face to build trust and discern what's important to them.

Build personal rapport. Talk freely about personal connections you may have. Better yet, get them talking – about anything.

Build trust. Keep your promises – by showing up on time and providing information you said you'd give. Be prompt and reliable in your communications. This adds value to doing business with you. If possible, leverage the trust you've already built with others – preferably with mutual friends, but also with references or reviews.

Don't assume that money is always the top priority. Time is often a major factor – they may need the space or equipment or money right away. Your trustworthiness and ability to complete the deal can be a major factor. There are often other factors unique to the deal at hand.

Ask questions and listen to learn their priorities. "Listening is the most important part of any negotiation. Make sure you hear what is really being said. Develop the habit of questioning what you see on the surface and digging to find out what's really going on" (Norm Brodsky Street Smarts p.103).

Seek to meet at least some of their priorities while meeting your own. Negotiation is give and take.

Negotiate on a secondary priority, then give way to gain leverage on your top priority. See expert quote at beginning of chapter.

Gauge their sense of urgency. How badly does the other party want to do business with you? Observe their body language and tone of voice. Read other cues, such as when they show up, how much time they spend with you, and how much they try to win you over. Their sense of urgency is proportionate to the amount of concessions they'll give.

Be honest about shortcomings. If you're selling something with a major drawback, such as old age or high mileage, go ahead and acknowledge it, then share the factors that outweigh it.

Discuss value. Highlight the value of what you bring to the table. When sharing ways their offering doesn't fit exactly with your needs, don't over state it. This lowers your credibility as you obviously wouldn't be there if you saw no value in what they're offering.

Allow the other party to propose the price. You can learn a lot about the other party from the initial price they propose. Are they greedy, fair, bluffing, serious, or unrealistic? Plus, the one who proposes the price should expect a counter-offer.

If the price is too far beyond what you'd consider, don't even counter-offer – as long as they have a sense of urgency to deal with you. Give it some time and they may counter-offer themselves, giving you a more reasonable starting point to negotiate from.

Know ahead of time which conditions you'll be willing to walk away from. Leaving without a deal is a powerful negotiating tool, so don't be afraid to use it. This may be literally walking out without a deal, or just letting the communication stall until the other party moves into your range of possibility. When you walk away, make it clear what it will take to bring you back to the negotiating table.

Be ready to offer a concession in order to land your top priority. This could be a longer term, a higher volume, delivery of the equipment, or some other perk to sweeten the deal. Both parties should walk away feeling they got a good deal. After all, commercial transactions are voluntary agreements that are meant to be win-wins. Each party gives up excess value they have to receive value they need.

Ask for extras. Let them sweeten the deal for you. Sometimes they can give something extra without hurting themselves too much. For example, on a used piece of equipment, they may be willing to change the oil, fuel it up, and include a spare tire or accessory.

Pay a little more for quality. Get the best price you can, but consider the hidden high costs that come with low-quality products.

When you reach a deal, put it in writing. Include who's agreed to do what and when. Make sure both parties sign it and receive a copy. Promptly keep your end of the deal.

In adversarial negotiations:

1. If the other party thinks you owe them money, time is on your side. They'll likely be more flexible if you negotiate later.
2. Be ready to compromise. While a win-win is optimal, the best case scenario in adversarial negotiations is that both parties get some of what they want and accept some disappointment as well.

3. Weigh the emotional stress, mental distraction, and financial costs before going to court. Often the best course is to work it out between you without intermediaries.

Case Study

I recently sold a tractor for twice what we paid for it two years ago. A big part of that was the great price my brother negotiated from the customer who was eager to get rid of it. He had used it for a single driveway building project and even though selling it cheap, he still saved money by doing the project himself. Then, when I decided to sell it, I was able to get a great price for it because of its great condition and low hours. I had to overcome two big drawbacks with potential buyers: it was eight years old and it didn't have an enclosed, air-conditioned cab like most others available in the same model. I used many of the tactics I write about here. Quick and professional communication set me apart and built trust. The happy buyer said: "there's not many people out there who do business like you." I had two potential buyers and used that fact to show the value of my product and increase the sense of urgency. We had reached an impasse after haggling the price over the course of a week. We were $2,000 apart on a $33,000 piece of equipment. When my other potential buyer dropped out, I made a final concession that won my buyer over. I offered to pay the shipping if he met my latest counter-offer, since I had a shipping option that I knew was less than half of what he could ship it for. The $850 I paid in shipping bought me $2,000 in the deal, and he didn't have to go through the hassle of picking it up 1400 km away. Everyone was happy – as it should be!

Leading Self, Employees, Systems

SELF – Be careful what you say. Know what you want. Know your limits. Listen well. Help the deal work for the other party.

EMPLOYEES – Employees can do some of the research and preliminary negotiations for major deals, so you may want to share some of these negotiating skills with them. When they negotiate their salaries with you, consider the cost of hiring and training a replacement while also seeing their strengths and weaknesses clearly.

SYSTEMS – Comparison spreadsheets can help in the research phase of a major purchase. Written contracts are essential to ensure the terms of a deal are clear and enforceable.

NOW WHAT?

Summary

Know what you want from a deal, but instead of sharing all of those details, focus on listening and learning what is most important to the other party. Gauge their sense of urgency when you meet in person. Build rapport by letting them talk, then try to meet some of their priorities while receiving yours. Know when to walk away, counter-offer, or stand firm. Compromise when your sense of urgency to do the deal is stronger than theirs. Get the deal in writing and sign it.

Application Questions

1. Which of your expense categories will you seek better deals in?

2. What research do you need to do for your next major purchase?

3. Who are the top two suppliers of your next major purchase?

4. Which of the above people skills do you want to grow in?

5. Which of the above tactics do you want to try in your next deal?

Recommended Reading

Street Smarts by Norm Brodsky and Bo Burlingham

Make it Happen!

What ideas has this chapter stirred in me?

What new light does this chapter shine on my leadership and my business?

What changes do I plan to make?

My actions to *Make it Happen!*	Completion dates	
	Proposed	Actual

Chapter 20 | Access Capital & Limit Debt

By Evan Keller

WHAT?

Definition

Small businesses must be able to acquire the capital they need to grow while keeping overall debt load in proper proportion to company assets and revenue.

Expert Quote

"What is the 'appropriate' level of debt? This becomes a balancing act because you want to avoid excessive leverage and minimize cash outflows for debt servicing, but you also want to fuel growth and increase the return on the owner's investment….'What's best for your business' really is the only correct answer….It depends on your strategic objective, your personal attitude toward risk, the kind of business you operate, the size of your business, your cash flow dynamics, the volatility of your sales, your competitive situation, etc." (Michael Gerber, E-Myth Mastery p.204)

Assessment Questions

1. Are you able to get all the financing you need at attractive rates?

2. Do you have strong, long-term relationships with multiple lenders?

3. If you sold all your company real estate and equipment today at market value, would the proceeds pay off all your loans?

4. Does your balance sheet show positive equity? Do you have more equity than you did last year and the year before?

5. What is your debt-service ratio? (Calculate by: annual net operating income / annual total of debt payments).

6. Do you know your total current debt load?

7. What do you currently do to keep your debt under control?

8. Do you have a desire and plan to make your company debt-free?

WHY?

Benefits

Agility. Access to capital allows you to grow when opportunities present themselves or keep up with existing production when current equipment fails.

Increased capacity. Capital for equipment or raw materials allows you to fill more and larger orders.

Financial health. When you only take on necessary debt and pay it down diligently, your balance sheet will show strong company viability and valuation.

Barriers

Unprofitability. When your profit and loss statements (and tax returns) do not show a history of profitability, a bank will not loan to you. Can you blame them? Angry entrepreneurs often blame the lender, saying "banks aren't lending money."

Bad credit. Personal bankruptcies and foreclosures on your credit report (or your partner's) can disqualify you from traditional lenders for a period of time.

Runaway debt. If you're reckless in accumulating debt, you devalue your own company, cripple your cash flow, risk corporate bankruptcy, and undercut your chances of obtaining additional financing.

Underlying Values

Trust. It's about the relationship (and the numbers!). Lenders – like all people – want to do business with those they know and trust. If you demonstrate integrity and good business management over time, a lender may take a bigger risk on you than they normally would. – Proverbs 20:6-7

Discernment. Find out what investments increase the efficiency of your operations or lead to more high-margin sales. Avoid vanity purchases that do not grow your business, such as fancy cars and offices. – Proverbs 23:1-3

Restraint. It's wise to not take on more than you can handle. Grow slow and steady rather than overreaching and losing all you've built. "Nonfatal failure is encouraged and is how you learn to ride a bike. But when you borrow to implement your latest 'brilliant' plan, you exponentially increase your chances of fatal failure" (Dave Ramsey, Entreleadership p.196). – Proverbs 23:4

Foresight. Use break-even analysis, advice from your accountant, and conservative intuition to gauge whether new equipment purchases will more than pay for themselves.

Diligence. If you want lenders to provide more financing, then control your current debt, including paying off credit cards each month. When you sell equipment or real estate, use the entire proceeds to pay down long-term debt. – Ecclesiastes 5:4-5

HOW?

Steps to Implement

<u>Access Capital:</u>

1. **Increase your company's profitability.** This is the surest way to get a loan as it shows the bank you have

the ability to pay them back. Entrepreneurs often work with their accountants to show a year-end loss to minimize their tax burden. This strategy is often wise, but sometimes needs to be constrained by your need for loans. Another practice that reduces profitability is entrepreneurs paying personal expenses with company funds. This also looks unprofessional to the bankers you're trying to impress. Keep them separate.

2. **Establish long and trusting relationships with lenders, preferably local community banks with local decisions, excellent service, and limited bureaucracy.** Establish trust over time by being a good business and personal customer. Don't write bad checks and keep healthy checking and savings balances. Over a long period of time, this will build equity in the relationship that will serve you well when asking for a loan. Knowing bank officers on a personal basis will add to that trust (that is, if you demonstrate personal integrity). Even when you don't need a loan, meet with your banker at least quarterly, and keep them informed of big developments in your business.

3. **Meet with your accountant before asking for a loan.** Get advice on whether you can handle the loan you want (using break-even analysis and cash flow forecasting). Get help understanding your financials, including

trends in your profitability that may interest the bank. Know your own debt-service ratio and why it is what it is. Again, calculate by: annual net operating income / annual total of debt payments. Many banks will only loan you money if yours is 1.25 or higher.

4. **Have your financial affairs in orders when applying for a loan.** Be prepared to complete a personal financial statement, provide your two most recent personal and business tax returns, and provide the last two years of financial statements as well as year-to-date ones. Since the bank likely knows little of your business practices, they may read a lot into how slowly or quickly you are able to compile these. Slow, incomplete, or conflicting documents can raise your rate or kill your loan altogether.

5. **Use lines-of-credit properly.** Banks will be wary if your line-of-credit is always maxed out or is used for equipment, taxes, or regular monthly expenses.

6. **Close unneeded lines-of-credit.** If you've accumulated enough retained earnings, they can serve as your own in-house line of credit, allowing you to close the one that charges rather than pays interest. This will help your term loan chances since lenders will often assume a maxed out line-of-credit when calculating your ability to pay back the loan you're applying for. Closing lines-of-

credit you no longer need is a great way to get debt off your books.

7. **Build up your store of retained earnings.** Lenders see this as another potential source of paying back their loan. See chapter 17.

8. **Clean up your personal credit, if possible.** If there is an unjust negative entry on your credit report, offer documentation to explain it.

9. **If you've not established trust with the lender you're applying to, provide strong credit references with suppliers you've done business with for a while.** Offer these before they even ask for them!

10. **If the bank says "no" after taking all of the above steps, make sure you understand exactly why, and under what conditions they would have said "yes."** Don't let your frustration harm the relationship you may need later. Instead, take it as constructive criticism to make corrections in your business that will make it stronger.

11. If traditional banks won't lend to you, and you're still convinced you're ready for a new loan, there are other alternatives, including:

    - Industry-specific lenders – These folks know your industry and understand some of the peculiars of your situation, so they can read your risk factors better than some banks.

- Manufacturer financing – You can often buy new equipment or vehicles directly from the manufacturer at lower rates than traditional banks. Since they know their collateral better than the average bank, they may approach a risky client differently.

- SBA loans – These government-backed loans reduce risks to banks and credit unions, allowing them to make loans they wouldn't offer otherwise (to newer businesses or risky businesses such as restaurants). They have low rates and long terms, but have heavy stipulations, and require lots of time and paperwork. Take one only as a last resort. See the case study below for more.

- Peer-to-peer lending – Interest rates are higher than traditional lenders, but are easier to qualify for, although you may need to start with a smaller loan than you'd like.

- Venture capitalists, angel investors, personally known investors – Information on these is plenteous and beyond the scope of this book, so I'll be brief. Down sides are that they will want an equity share in your company, require a rigorous process, and a closer relationship – including a say in the direction of your company. On the plus side, they can infuse huge amounts of capital that are sometimes needed for product development or explosive growth. This is one of those defining forks in the road. Building a business without loans means slower growth, but I can tell you there's nothing like being forced to be profitable from day one. I started my business with no capital and borrowed tools that all broke on the first job, but that kept me scrappy. Jason Fried says this about his large company: "…dozens of venture capitalists and private equity firms have offered us lots of money. Instead, my customers have always been my investors. My goal has always been to be profitable on Day One….[Outside funding] replaces the hustle, the scrap, the fight, with a false comfort of 'we can worry about that later.'" ("How to Get Good at Making Money," Inc Magazine, March 2011, p.60, http://www.inc.com/magazine/20110301/making-money-small-business-advice-from-jason-fried.html).

- Family and friends – I put this last because it complicates personal relationships.

Limit Debt:

1. **Know your current total debt load** (using a spreadsheet as described below in "Systems").

2. **Avoid unnecessary purchases.** Get good advice and try short-term rentals first.

3. **Negotiate good deals on everything you buy** – see chapter 19.

4. **Buy with your retained earnings rather than a loan when possible.** Plan for large purchases by saving from your internal cash flow – see chapter 17.

5. **Shop interest rates and origination fees amongst your lenders.** On a $100,000 loan over four years, you pay roughly $4,500 more for an 8% loan compared to a 6% one. Caveat: I'd pay up to 1% more to a lender whom I have a strong relationship with, and is easy to work with.

6. **Ensure your loan term doesn't outlast the value of its collateral.** Don't get a six year loan on equipment that loses most of its value in four. If you still owe money on

it when it outlasts it value to you, selling will be complicated by the fact that the bank holds its title.

7. **Get the shortest term (yes, the highest payment!) your cash flow can handle.** On a $100,000 loan at 6%, you pay roughly double the interest over six years compared to three years. More importantly, the shorter term will free up cash flow for future equipment needs. Caveat: the higher payment of a shorter term hurts your debt-service ratio more (but for a shorter period of time).

8. **Make a substantial down payment if your cash flow can handle it.** If you're company is not yet cash flow positive, you'll want to take the opposite approach on this and the previous step.

9. **Pay down long-term debt with all proceeds from sales of no-longer-needed equipment and real estate.** Be disciplined in this. The only exception should be reinvesting in new equipment purchases.

10. **Pay down long-term debt with unexpected surpluses** (as long as it doesn't threaten your cash flow).

11. **Pay *down* the highest-rate loans first.** That is, unless you need to free up cash flow (and raise debt-service ratio) by paying *off* the lowest balance loan(s).

12. **Limit your own pay until you have positive equity and are able to secure all the financing you need.**

13. **Buy new when the bank won't finance used equipment, when the manufacturer offers excellent rates or needed warranties, or when maintenance costs on used equipment outweigh the price savings.**

14. **Buy used when new equipment depreciates too rapidly or is subject to additional taxes.** Buy only late model used equipment so that maintenance costs are low. Start looking long before you need it since late model used equipment can be hard to find.

15. **Consider leasing instead of buying, especially if you don't need the equipment or real estate long-term.** Other reasons include avoiding debt or taking advantage of low leasing rates. If you can't afford to buy new equipment, leasing new equipment will cost you less in maintenance than buying old equipment.

16. **Outsource functions that require additional equipment, and then buy the equipment later when you can afford it.** Or – especially if they don't help produce your core products or services – continue subcontracting out those functions to others who own such equipment.

17. **Pay off your business credit card every month.** It likely has a higher interest rate than your other loans. It took

several years for my business to reach this goal; it is possible!

Case Study

When my company was 11 years old, I was still driving a truck that was just as old. When asked why I bought new dump trucks for the crew, but drive an old pickup myself, I replied: "I've got to take care of my baby now so it will take good care of me later."

Now that, we built up some cash reserves (as advised in chapter 17), I closed our line of credit and cover any large unexpected expenses from our own retained earnings. Since being cash flow positive has eliminated the need to minimize monthly payment amounts, I started getting 24-36 month equipment loans instead of 60 month terms.

That helped us control our debt load while buying 5-8 pieces of heavy equipment each year. In our 10th year, we began buying all brand new equipment – dumping 15-year-old dump trucks for new $120,000 ones. After years of paying off most of our loans early, our next milestone will be to pay off *all* of our company debt, which we're on schedule to accomplish by year 15. Then we'll be our own bank! Now that's freedom.

Leading Self, Employees, Systems

SELF – Make these important financial decisions and initiatives with advice from your accountant. Only take loans that have an excellent chance of growing your company and be diligent in paying down debt.

EMPLOYEES – Make sure your office personnel pay your loans on time and provide you with accurate financial reports regularly.

SYSTEMS – Make a spreadsheet of all your debt, complete with loan amount, current balance, and monthly payment. Include dates of origination, maturation, monthly payment, interest rate, term, lender, loan number, and collateral. Use this to keep a running total of your overall debt load and to quickly compare rates and terms amongst lenders. You can see at a glance when an upcoming payoff will increase your cash flow. Another reason to create this spreadsheet is that potential lenders will ask for a list of your debt payments in order to calculate your debt-service ratio.

NOW WHAT?

Summary

Gain access to capital by building a history of profitability, managing your credit history, knowing your pertinent financial ratios with your accountant's help, nurturing strong banking relationships, and providing current financials and tax returns. If your loan requests are denied, fix the problems in your business and explore non-traditional lenders. Limit debt by knowing your debt load, avoiding unnecessary loans, getting low rates and short terms, and diligently paying down your loans – early if possible. Decide whether your company should work towards becoming completely debt-free. These steps will add to the agility, capacity, and financial health of your business.

Application Questions

1. Which of the above steps to accessing capital will you take?
2. Which of the above steps to limiting debt will you take?
3. How might you want to shift your attitude about bankers towards a more constructive posture?
4. What major purchases will you need to make over the next year? What is your tax strategy?
5. What loans do you hope to pay off next? Is it feasible to pay off all your debt?
6. Are you getting what you need from your current accountant and bookkeeper?
7. Which types of non-traditional lenders would be worth exploring?

Recommended Reading

Street Smarts by Norm Brodsky

Make it Happen!

What ideas has this chapter stirred in me?

What new light does this chapter shine on my leadership and my business?

What changes do I plan to make?

My actions to *Make it Happen!*	Completion dates	
	Proposed	Actual

Chapter 21 | Manage Major Risks

By Evan Keller

WHAT?

Definition

As your company becomes more and more successful, you have more and more to lose. Seemingly small oversights can put your years of investment at risk. Several small but important steps to identify and manage those risks will increase your peace of mind and guard against a crippling loss.

Expert Quote

"Be fully aware of the condition of your flock, and pay close attention to your herds. Wealth is not forever; nor does a crown last from one generation to the next." – Proverbs 27:23-24, by King Solomon, one of the ancient world's wealthiest people.

Assessment Questions

1. What risks are you already managing well?
2. What has kept you from focusing on reducing the major remaining risks?
3. What unaddressed concerns do your family members and business partner have?

WHY?

Benefits

Peace of mind. You'll sleep better at night knowing that you're not one accident or lawsuit away from bankruptcy.

Peaceful relations. When agreements are in writing, trust can overtake suspicion in various working relationships.

Confidence. You can take wise risks to expand when ominous threats are managed well.

Wealth creation. Whereas risk management costs money, it can keep the economic engine functioning even when disaster strikes.

Barriers

Procrastination. Many things we know we need to do are displaced by the "tyranny of the urgent." Written policies and contracts take time and mental focus.

Cost. Insurance and lawyers cost money – often lots of it.

The unknown. We're unaware of some major risks until it's too late.

Complexity. Operating agreements can be daunting to understand and compose.

Informality. We are tempted to leave some important arrangements to verbal agreements, but handshake goodwill can wear thin when financial or relational adversity strikes.

Underlying Values

Wisdom. Protecting your biggest investment is a no-brainer. – Proverbs 3:21-26

Responsibility. Your family and employees are depending on you to protect their livelihoods.

Caution. Your optimism needs to be tempered by realism about human depravity and a world where things often go wrong. – Mathew 10:16

Compliance. As hard as that word is for this renegade entrepreneur to write, disregarding the law can bring harsh penalties on top of being a bad example. – Romans 13:1

Vision. Seeing future possibilities should influence what you focus on today. – Proverbs 31:25-27

HOW?

Steps to Implement

Identify your major vulnerabilities using these questions:

EQUIPMENT/PROPERTY

1. Do you have proper insurance on all vehicles and equipment from the very first to the very last day they are in service?

2. Do you maintain all equipment and vehicles for safe usage?

3. Do you need to acquire newer equipment to reduce the risk of accident?

4. Is your real estate insured for all types of losses?

5. Do you have emergency contingency plans, especially for natural disasters that your location is prone to? Are trees near your buildings healthy and properly pruned? (As any good tree guy would ask!)

6. Do you have a backup power source, such as a generator, if your operations depend heavily on electricity?

7. Do you secure all physical property properly, with: locks, cameras, fences, security and GPS tracking systems?

8. Do you change locks when an employee is terminated?

9. How do you ensure that failure of a new location (or product) will not cripple your entire business?

10. Do you keep titles, laptops, not-yet-deposited cash, and sensitive product information in a fireproof safe?

EMPLOYEES

1. Do you perform background checks on potential employees?

2. Do you have a written substance abuse policy and is it enforced with pre-employment, post-accident, and random drug screenings?

3. Do you have a written safety policy, ongoing safety training, random safety checks, and documented safety committee meetings at least quarterly (in manual labor industries)?

4. Are your employee policies compiled in a manual, and do you have a signed statement of agreement from each employee acknowledging that they have received and read them?

5. Do you make sure to follow all anti-discrimination laws with your employees and customers?

1. Do you closely guard any trade secrets that would help competitors reduce your competitive advantage?

6. Have your employees signed non-compete agreements?

7. Is your business overly dependent on a single employee? What can you do to train others to handle various parts of this person's job?

8. Do you do regular inventory checks to prevent theft?

9. Have you expressed a zero tolerance policy for using company equipment and products for personal use without permission?

10. Do you reconcile cash daily?

11. Have you implemented separation of duties (see chapter 18) to reduce internal fraud?

12. Do you ensure that all subcontractors are fully insured?

13. Do you have a signed hold harmless agreement with each subcontractor?

CUSTOMERS

1. Do you use written contracts for all major customers, suppliers, and subcontractors?

2. Do you extend significant credit only to trusted customers or to those you've vetted and received a sizeable deposit from?

3. Are you overly reliant on a small number of customers or vendors? How can you diversify?

4. Could customers quickly lose interest in your main product line?

5. Do you use liability releases for all liabilities that your customers may be exposed to?

6. Do you have enough liability coverage for the size of your company and the type of industry you're in?

7. Do you respond quickly to resolve any major customer complaints in order to minimize lawsuits?

8. Do you regularly monitor your online reputation?

PARTNERS

1. If you have one or more partners, do you have a signed and notarized operating agreement that stipulates everything from percentage of ownership to assigned duties to compensation to separation – including contingencies for death and divorce?

2. Do you have a written succession plan if you are planning to retire and pass on the business to a partner or family member?

3. Do you have sizeable life insurance policies on all owners any "key" employees who would be hard to replace?

4. Do you have disability and health insurance for all owners?

5. Do you have an up-to-date will and a durable power of attorney?

1. Do you take measures to prevent identity theft?

FINANCE

1. Is 100% of your payroll "on the books", including bonuses?

2. Do you report all your revenue and pay your taxes? Do you maintain appropriate records? How would you fare in an IRS audit?

3. Do you engage in tax planning to avoid a major surprise tax burden?

4. Do you plan your equipment purchases in order to maximize Section 179 deductions?

5. Do you audit payroll periodically to ensure hours are being reported honestly?

6. Do you monitor all employee spending – especially company credit cards – and have proper checks and balances in place?

7. Do you avoid using debit cards since they are less secure than credit cards?

8. Do you limit signers on your business checking account?

9. Do you have enough in savings and accessible investments to cover three months of operating expenses should you experience a major cash flow crisis?

10. Do you make sure you don't grow so fast that your cash flow cannot cover increased production costs until payments from new sales come in?

11. Do you have an excessive debt-to-equity ratio?

TECHNOLOGY

1. Do you protect your important financial passwords?
2. Do you change the passwords when someone with access to them leaves the company?
3. Do you have adequate firewall and virus protection?
4. Do you protect your intellectual property with appropriate trademarks and patents?
5. Do you limit access to your website FTP and financial accounts? Do you vary the level of access by job duty?
6. Do you own URLs similar to your own to guard against copycats and misspellings?
7. Is your website URL is on auto-renew so it can never be high-jacked for ransom?
8. Do you keep your customers' credit card information secure (whether online or otherwise)? If you keep this data on file, do you have cyber insurance to cover data breaches?
9. Do you shred all sensitive information that is being discarded?
10. Do you have all your data backed up online?

Consult appropriate experts on the risks that concern you most, including bankers, accountants, attorneys, financial planners, and insurance agents.

Determine which risks are the largest and have a higher probability of occurring.

Prioritize and schedule the ones you'll address. Mobilize yourself, your employees, and outside experts as needed to implement risk management strategies. Action will take many forms, including purchasing insurance, crafting policies, entering into contracts, and enacting procedures. Communicate as needed to all who are affected by the changes you make, helping them see the benefits of your status quo disruptions.

Case Study

In Tree Work Now's early years, I tried out a new worker, planning to add him to the payroll after seeing if he had the right skills and work ethic. My delay negated his being covered by our Workers' Compensation policy when he fell out of a tree and broke his leg that first week. Of course, he sued my business and the insurance company. This began an 18-month headache for me, filled with depositions, court appearances, those dreaded certified letters, and insomnia. At least I enjoyed giving a closing argument in which I chastised the defendant's lawyer for taking on such a frivolous case - since the employee tested positive for cocaine after his fall. (We won the case.) This reveals another mistake. Although we had a drug-free policy, we didn't do pre-employment drug testing – something we promptly corrected.

Leading Self, Employees, Systems

SELF – Don't be overwhelmed by the number potential liabilities. Rather channel that fear into clear-minded prioritization and quick action. Risk management isn't your most exciting role, so it takes extra intentionality. Being a risk taker doesn't give you license to be reckless.

EMPLOYEES – Many areas of risk management involve protecting you from employees, protecting employees from risks, and enlisting their help in reducing various vulnerabilities. So, communicate your expectations and acknowledge their positive contributions.

SYSTEMS – Types of needed systems include employee policies, financial procedures, contracts, and regular checkups on a variety of operations that could go south without attention.

NOW WHAT?

Summary

Managing major risks can improve profitability, morale, and peace of mind. It's the wise and responsible thing to do – a prime example of working "on", not "in" your business. Your biggest vulnerabilities may be related to equipment/property, employees, customers, partners, finance, or technology. Once you've identified your major risks, consult the experts, determine the size and probability of the risks, prioritize and schedule your interventions, then enact and communicate your solutions.

Application Questions

1. Which of these categories of risk are you most vulnerable in: equipment/property, employees, customers, partners, finance, or technology?

2. Using the many questions in the "Steps to Implement" section, which risks do you need to better manage?

3. Which exposures to liability will you shore up this year? Which will you address next year?

4. Which experts do you need to consult?

5. Which partners and employees do you need to enlist to formulate and implement your risk management plan?

Recommended Reading

Small Business Risk Management Resources from SBDC: www2.lsbdc.org/Documentmaster.aspx?doc=2313

Risk Management for Small Businesses by Manoj Jain

Make it Happen!

What ideas has this chapter stirred in me?

What new light does this chapter shine on my leadership and my business?

What changes do I plan to make?

My actions to *Make it Happen!*	Completion dates	
	Proposed	Actual

Chapter 22 | Resist Corruption

By Evan Keller, largely adapted from the Corruption Toolkit at businessasmission.com, with permission.

WHAT?

Definition

"Corruption is defined as the misuse of power by someone to whom it has been entrusted, for their own private gain. The most common form of corruption is bribery, which is defined as the giving or receiving of money, a gift or other advantage as an inducement to do something that is dishonest, illegal or a breach of trust in the course of doing business." – Transparency International's "Business Principles for Countering Bribery: Small and Medium Enterprise Edition"

Expert Quote

"Ethics may be defined as the moral philosophy of knowing the difference between what is right and wrong and acting accordingly. It includes a moral duty and obligation to do good….Ethics has its root in the Greek word "ethos" which means character; therefore an ethical framework is a systematic set of concepts which provides guidelines for correct behaviour that demonstrates ideal individual and corporate character." – Larry Sharp "Guidelines for Cross-Cultural Business Ethics", http://businessasmission.com/guidelines-business-ethics/

Assessment Questions

1. What unethical actions have you been asked to take in the last year?

2. What are the likely consequences of never paying a bribe?

3. Have you prepared your employees to prevent and respond to unethical demands?

WHY?

Benefits

Clear conscience. Doing the right thing is good for your mental and spiritual wellbeing. It strengthens your character, especially if standing for good is costly.

Lack of escalation. Once you're known to comply with unethical demands, those demands will increase in frequency and amount, with potential to bankrupt your business. On the other hand, if you refuse to give in to such demands, it could cost you a lot in the short term, but will likely save you money in the long-term as fewer people will waste their time making unethical demands of you.

Agent of change. Others may follow your example as you show them how resisting corruption can be done profitably. Standing against corruption may increase your influence as seen in the case study below.

Barriers

Loss of money. Losing a deal or government permission to do business can be very costly.

Loss of time. Delays on bureaucratic processes or business deals often translate into loss of profit.

Loss of life. Organized crime uses threats of violence in their extortion schemes.

Underlying Values

Accountability to God. "Fyodor Dostoyevsky prophetically wrote: 'if there is no God, then everything is permissible. Crime will be inevitable.' Atheism removed the basis of personal responsibility and accountability for behavior before God as well as society. Atheism removed any higher moral authority than one's own. The natural consequence is the mentality of 'every man for himself' and 'survival of the fittest', rather than by principle and rule of law." - Kevin White, Kazakhstan Country Director for the Religious Freedom and Business Foundation, http://businessasmission.com/worldview-implications-kazakhstan/ - 2 Corinthians 5:10

Emulation of Christ. As followers of Jesus, we are called to embody his grace, truth, and righteousness. This will lead to both suffering and glory as we become more like him, which is God's very purpose for us. – Romans 8:17

Advocacy for the poor. Corruption often involves the powerful oppressing the poor, something God hates and promises to judge. – Isaiah 1:23

Principles over profit. While a business needs to be profitable to stay in business, we should have higher values than *maximizing* profit.

Dependence on God. While corrupt people seek to leverage their power over us, we must continually remind ourselves that God can even bring good out of their evil. God alone is in control and is our ultimate, gracious provider. – Matthew 6:25-33

Fearlessness. When you stand against a corrupt system, you will make enemies. Maxime Pierre of Partners Worldwide in Haiti says "Don't mind having enemies; corrupt enemies reveal your integrity." He told me of a time his pastor spoke publicly against corrupt government officials and false accusations were circulated about him shortly thereafter. Hundreds protested peacefully in support of him; the public knew who was corrupt and who wasn't. – Psalm 27:1

HOW?

Steps to Implement

Find creative business solutions. Refusing to pay a bribe may stall bureaucratic approvals or supplier transactions. Extortion is also a major issue in some places. Many of our business friends in Honduras have to be discreet about publishing their phone numbers or displaying their faces in their marketing materials. For example, because gangs were calling, threatening violence if Mayte didn't pay the "war tax," she felt compelled to remove her phone number from the sign in front of her beauty salon in Tegucigalpa. Instead, she's employed a variety of other ways to connect with potential clients and continue to grow her business. So, when corruption strikes, take it as an opportunity to fully engage your creativity to advance your company despite that challenge. Perhaps this is one way God will bring good out of evil.

Be strong. Bribery thrives on pressure – on your time and money. Extortion thrives on fear and intimidation. In both cases, perpetrators are looking for easy targets and will likely look for other victims when you resist. "Do not be overcome by evil" (Romans 12:21). Do take reasonable precautions against credible threats.

Prepare your employees. Start by writing and explaining good policies. Have them sign a code of conduct each year committing to them.

Prevent and respond to demands. The RESIST publication (see recommended reading below) gives detailed guidance for both – including general practices (in appendix) and specific application to 22 common corruption scenarios.

Scrutinize potentially corrupt proposals. To apply the "Golden Rule", Dwight Nordstrom suggests you "practice 'reverse role-playing': put yourself in the role of each party involved in the deal. If you are the potential 'seller' in the proposed action, reverse the roles and become the 'buyer'. When you play the roles, put yourself in the place of the top manager of the other party and ask yourself if you like what the proposed action will do to your company. Do you have any negative feelings now concerning the proposed action?" – Pacific Resources International's Corruption Prevention Practices: 4 Step Process

Withdraw. Refuse to go through with transactions that violate the law, your company policies, and the "Golden Rule."

Work with authorities against corruption. Disclose specific corrupt demands, encourage passing of good anti-corruption laws, and the enforcement of those laws.

Case Study

Turbocam manufactures turbine parts using a precision engineering technique called 5-axis machining. The 5-axis technique uses computer-controlled milling machines that move and tilt both the part being cut and the cutting tool itself on 5 different axes. This level of precision enables the machining of very intricate shapes and the machines required are extremely complex, involving delicate mechanical and electrical components.

In 1993, a full four years after founding, Turbocam India finally had all the paperwork it needed to import its first 5-axis machine. Upon its arrival in India, the machine was then held up in Customs at Bombay Airport with its delicate components exposed to the elements. Knowing the machine would likely be ruined by the humid climate, Duncan felt under pressure by demands to 'oil the wheels' of Bombay Customs with the payment of a bribe. One night, as things were coming to a head and the way forward did not seem obvious, Duncan's wife encouraged him, 'Why don't you ask the Lord what you should do?' Opening the Bible to his daily reading for that day, Duncan was quite sure that he had his answer when he read the words of Job 15 verse 34; 'For the company of the godless will be barren, and fire will consume the tents of those who love bribes.' So the company stood firm on their core value of not paying bribes and waited for 3 months before their machine was released. As he feared, the machine was badly damaged, but decades later, Turbocam has grown in business success and as a catalyst for others in the fight against corruption. Many people have said it is impossible to do what they have done and yet they are still doing it. Just a few years ago they had to wait for 16 different permits to set up a new factory on land in Goa and despite the extra costs incurred they stood firm in their convictions to never pay a bribe. Now they are having a ripple effect as they share their story. Their company history has earned them a voice in the public square and they are using it.

Corruption is one of the hottest topics for debate in Indian society, with sporadic nationwide protests and Anti-corruption Legislation consistently stalled in the Indian political process. In this climate, those in the company have been able to share the Turbocam story and it has opened doors to be able to influence in the public arena. The Times of India newspaper ran a couple of features on Turbocam's no bribe policy and back in Goa, Savio noticed the after-effects of those articles when the President of the industrial estate where the Turbocam plant is located forwarded copies to all the other businesses in the estate saying, 'This is one of our own, now we need to act like this as a group!' Both Duncan and Marian have received a prestigious "Karmaveer Puraskaar" the Global Awards for Citizen Action and Social Justice. See the full story by Jo Plummer at: http://businessasmission.com/turbocam-india/

Leading Self, Employees, Systems

SELF – Set the standard high. Your company will only be as ethical as you are. Some things are more important than money and efficiency. God sees, and he's your provider.

EMPLOYEES – Expect complete transparency, avoid cash payments, and require approval before giving any gifts necessary to gain business or get something done.

SYSTEMS – Implement segregation of duties (see chapter 18) to reduce internal fraud. Have a written policy for dealing with bribery and extortion, and include anti-corruption clauses in your contracts.

NOW WHAT?

Summary

Resisting corruption requires equally taxing doses of emotional resilience and due diligence. Doing the right thing is often costly in the short-term, but is true to values that are higher than profit.

―― BUSINESS AS MISSION CHEAT SHEETS ――

6 Things When Faced With...

CORRUPTION

BE CLEAR — Have I made a clear, public commitment to integrity? Do I have policies that back that up?

BE LEGAL — Does this action violate any law? Do I know the law as it applies to my business context?

BE TRANSPARENT — Is this deal transparent to all parties? Can I make this transaction openly?

BE ACCOUNTABLE — Can this transaction be documented in some way? Would it stand up to audit?

BE CERTAIN — Can I proudly tell others about this action? Is my gut feeling or conscience telling me no?

BE BIBLICAL — Do I align with the Bible's teaching on bribery? Are my actions a good witness for Christ?

→→→ KEEP ME. PRINT ME. ←←←

BUSINESSASMISSION.COM

Application Questions

1. What are the consequences of various responses to this proposed action?

2. Is the proposed action transparent to all involved parties?

3. Does the proposed action violate the law?

4. Does the proposed action pass Rotary International's "Four Way Test"? We recite these four questions at Rotary every Thursday morning: "Is it the truth? Is it fair to all concerned? Will it build goodwill and better friendships? Will it be beneficial to all concerned?"

5. Is the proposed action based on greed and does it oppress the powerless?

6. Does the proposed action "pervert the course of justice" (Proverbs 17:23)?

7. Does the proposed action reflect the "Golden Rule" to "do to others as you want them to do to you" (Matthew 7:12)?

Recommended Reading

"Business Principles for Countering Bribery" by Transparency International

"RESIST - Resisting Extortion and Solicitation in International Transactions" by International Chamber of Commerce, Transparency International, United Nations Global Compact, and World Economic Forum.

Make it Happen!

What ideas has this chapter stirred in me?

What new light does this chapter shine on my leadership and my business?

What changes do I plan to make?

My actions to *Make it Happen!*	Completion dates	
	Proposed	Actual

Circle the appropriate action for each topic:

16. Achieve Positive Cash Flow - *Am I practicing effective cash flow management, and building systems to prevent future cash flow crises?*

    Maintain   Fine-Tune   Overhaul

17. Save Money Diligently - *Am I regularly saving as much as I can in a separate account, patiently building financial strength?*

    Maintain   Fine-Tune   Overhaul

18. Control Spending Closely - *Am I becoming more efficient by tracking my expenses and monitoring employee purchases?*

    Maintain   Fine-Tune   Overhaul

19. Negotiate Good Deals - *Do I negotiate great deals by learning what is important to the other party, building trust, and seeking to achieve my top priorities while meeting some of theirs?*

    Maintain   Fine-Tune   Overhaul

20. Access Capital & Limit Debt - *Am I gaining access to capital by being profitable, controlling debt, and providing documentation to lenders? Do I avoid unnecessary loans and pay down my loans as quickly as possible?*

    Maintain   Fine-Tune   Overhaul

21. Manage Major Risks - *Have I identified and managed my major risks related to property, employees, and customers?*

    Maintain   Fine-Tune   Overhaul

22. Resist Corruption - *Have you written policies and procedures so your employees know how to respond to unethical demands? Do you resist corruption even when it's costly?*

    Maintain   Fine-Tune   Overhaul

MY #1 FOCUS: _____

7. Giving Back

Use all you've been given to benefit others — serving employees, entrepreneurs, community and world. Therein your time, talent and treasure will find their true purpose and joy.

Chapter 23 | Help Employees Grow
By Mano De La Vega & Grace John

WHAT?

Definition

Employee development involves an ongoing assessment of your employees' skills and aspirations – aiming to optimize both. Helping employees grow as people is important because people matter. It will show that you care and will deepen those relationships. It will benefit your company, improve their personal lives, and prepare them for future roles inside or outside your company.

Expert Quote

"Most employers are trying to extract value from their people. If you foster dreams, you'll be adding value to their lives" (Mark Miller, <u>Chess Not Checkers</u>, p. 82).

Assessment Questions

1. How have you helped employees grow?
2. Have you identified employees with capacity to grow beyond their current role?
3. What investments are you making in employees, so that they remain committed to your business for the long term?
4. Do employees value you beyond their paycheck?
5. How has your attention or inattention to employees' families and interests affected your relationships to them and their work for you?
6. Are you disconnected from the personal lives of your employees? What are the pros and cons of that approach?

WHY?

Benefits

Maturity. People who are growing will be better family members, employees, and citizens.

Gratitude. As you take a genuine interest in their future and help them take steps forward, both of you will appreciate the relationship more.

Increased productivity. Taking an honest interest in someone builds loyalty. Loyal employees are more engaged. Engaged employees are more productive. Care for them and they may care for your company. These are the employees who give the extra effort, work the extra hour, or come up with your next big idea because they are committed to growing your business. Also, investing in these relationships can make it easier when you have to confront them or ask them to produce more on the job.

Increased influence. As you give more to others, they'll want to support what's important to you. This grows your capacity as a leader, strengthening your team to accomplish your business and nonprofit initiatives.

Fulfilment. It's satisfying to see an employee prosper because of your guidance.

Growth from the inside. Growing teams from within costs less than hiring from the outside.

Barriers

Task orientation. We often are so in a hurry to do the task at hand that we ignore people.

Lack of concern. Do you truly care about your employees or only what they can do for you?

Relational boundaries. You may fear becoming too familiar and losing your professional influence. Although it may be impossible to develop true peer-to-peer friendships with your employees, they'll actually respect you more if you invest in their personal as well as professional development.

Limited Resources. Don't allow financial constraints to keep you from investing in your employees. You'll inhibit the long-term growth of your business if you don't develop your people.

Underlying Values

People matter. People and meaningful relationships between them are of ultimate importance. C.S. Lewis reorients our perspective: "There are no ordinary people. You have never talked to a mere mortal. Nations, cultures, arts, civilizations - these are mortal, and their life is to ours as the life of a gnat" (C. S. Lewis, <u>The Weight of Glory</u> p. 45-46). – 1 Peter 5:2-3

Pay it forward. Just as several people have used their experience to shape you, share with employees how your inner growth led to your outer success. – 1 Peter 2:2

Legacy. The mark of a great leader is what you leave behind. Invest in what last – people.

HOW?

Steps to Implement

Assess talent. While this chapter focuses on personal development, don't forget professional development as discussed in chapter 15. Envision your employees' career potential. Discern which skills need more developing and provide opportunities for them to be refined.

Be curious. Ask about their families and interests. Know their family members names and what they like to do in their spare time. Remember and revisit what they share with you. If it's hard for you to remember such things, take notes that you can refer back to.

Provide personal support. While being careful to maintain appropriate boundaries, be available to support your employees with personal and family issues that they choose to share with you.

Be thoughtful. Give birthday gifts and notes of appreciation. Applaud wedding and work anniversaries, and other milestones that are important to them.

Listen. You're tuned in to the needs of your business; it takes extra intentionality to tune in to your employees. Ask open ended questions and let them talk without interruption. You'll learn some valuable things about both them and your company. You may even find that their aspirations can meet a need in your business.

Help raise their capacity. Give them books on subjects they'd like to grow in. Help them attend seminars and classes to help them learn, grow, and earn certifications.

Honor their privacy. If they'd rather keep their personal lives to themselves, honor that. You'll have more personal influence with certain employees, and that's okay.

Don't discriminate. While you'll naturally invest more in higher potential employees, there are legal requirements that certain programs be made available to all employees, or all who meet certain criteria (length of tenure, full-time, etc).

Invest in their physical health. Whether or not you're able to offer health insurance yet, wellness programs can increase employee engagement and retention. Programs can focus on weight-loss, nutrition, exercise, or tobacco cessation. Since insurance carriers can charge smokers more for health insurance, quitting can be a win-win for you and your employees. Obviously, be sensitive in how you address these issues, focusing on their felt needs.

Invest in their financial health. Connect your employees to financial information and services that will help them to increase savings, manage debt, and plan for their future. This is important in nurturing the long-term thinking and delayed gratification that is so vital to success in life. Knowing they are building long-term wealth can make today's hard work more bearable. You can also help them save money towards a matching year-end bonus as described in the case study in chapter 17.

Support their dreams. (See expert quote at beginning of this chapter.) They know you truly care when you help them toward dreams that may not benefit your company. Even better if you can benefit both, such as the mortgage assistance program mentioned in chapter one. Here's how it works: to assist high-performing employees in purchasing (or paying down) a home, Tree Work Now Inc matches dollar-for-dollar a maximum of $2,000 per year and $10,000 total towards the down payment of a home mortgage. This benefit reinforces long-term thinking, family stability, and employee loyalty and longevity. It also promotes high performance since the match amount is based on performance review scores.

Encourage them to set their own personal goals. In addition to health and financial goals, they may want to make changes in their family, career, education, or community involvement. They may want to grow emotionally, spiritually, or mentally. They may not be accustomed to setting or pursuing goals, so you could read chapter 3 with them.

Help them see their own potential. If you outperformed your own expectations for yourself, how did your horizons of possibility grow? Perhaps it was seeing a peer begin to excel, or maybe someone challenged you to greatness. As someone they hopefully respect, you are in a position to point out their potential. Challenge them to grow. Point out the achievements they've made thus far and help them see the potential you saw when you hired them. Build their confidence and support them as they pursue their goals. You can use Tony Robbins' "Strategy-Story-State" tool to help your employees re-write their stories and overcome longstanding barriers. See: http://sourcesofinsight.com/change-your-strategy-change-your-story-change-your-state/.

Bring in the experts. Bolster their goals with strategies from financial advisors, life coaches, nutritionists, personal trainers, etc. Provide group seminars at company meetings, then offer to pay all or part of the cost of individual follow up meetings for employees who want to go further.

Encourage accountability and support for their goals. They'll need this momentum to follow through. Encourage them to choose someone to keep them accountable for their personal goals at least quarterly. It may or may not be you. If you have to push them a lot to complete job-related initiatives, someone else might the be best to push them personally.

Case Study 1

I (Mano) remember when Ashley came to work at our restaurant – the second job in her young life. So, lacking in confidence, she said in her interview that she wasn't sure she could do the job. But I sensed that she could – if her confidence grew. She grew in many ways as we invested in her until she left for college. Two years later, she wrote us this letter:

> I just wanted to thank you for what I gained during my time working as a server at De La Vega a couple of years ago. Even though I was only part of the team for a few months, I learned so much through the experience. I was so intrigued by the family atmosphere and unique culture at the restaurant that I decided to write my college thesis on the topic of company culture. Thank you for sharing with me how you formed your core values from those of Zappos.com. I continued my research and realized that Zappos is a place I would really love to work one day because the company values and goals match my own. So I applied after graduating in May, and next week I will be moving to Las Vegas to work at Zappos headquarters as a Merchandising Assistant. "Gratitude is your daily

attitude" [a restaurant core value] has stuck with me and I wanted to reach out and thank you for inspiring me.

Have a great and busy weekend,
Ashley Kasevich

This is a great example of how our company values and our efforts to develop our employees paid off. She was clearly inspired to make a positive move that will benefit her personal life and career. That's what helping employees grow is all about.

Case Study 2

Isabel came to work for us when she turned 18 years old. In her interview, I (Mano) could tell she was a passionate person, and wanted to apply her creative energy in our kitchen. She had no kitchen skills whatsoever, but she was eager to learn and excel. She was open to constructive feedback and acted on it quickly. With regular coaching and a personal development plan, we were able to help Isabel improve her communication and kitchen skills to the point that she became our main prep chef. Isabel quickly became a key employee that other people relied on and looked up to.

Her passion never dwindled – even after being diagnosed with cancer while pregnant with her first child. The doctors thought it was impossible to save both mother and child, so Isabel and her husband were faced with the tough decision of choosing who they wanted to survive. But Isabel's fire and determination proved the doctors wrong. She was able to give birth to a beautiful baby girl, while she also survived the intense process of giving birth as her cancer accelerated.

As a company that values teamwork and good employee relationships, we all came together to raise funds for Isabel's cancer treatments. Her story and attitude inspired everyone around her, including family, friends, customers, hospital staff, and even complete strangers.

When her daughter Anisa was three years old, Isabel lost her battle against cancer. We'll always remember Isabel as a person who grew immensely as an outstanding employee, friend, mother, and inspiration to live with passion.

Leading Self, Employees, Systems

SELF – If you're like most hard-driving entrepreneurs, you may need to convince yourself that this is important. Developing employees starts with leading yourself well – see chapter 1.

EMPLOYEES – You can't invest equally in all, so invest most in your top leaders and potential leaders. Look for those who really want to grow and are receptive to your coaching. Have your employees write down their talents, goals, and aspirations. Continuously assess how you can connect your employees' skills to your company's needs.

SYSTEMS – In addition to the performance review process advised in chapter 15, schedule time to catch up with your employees personally. Make a system for recording and updating their progress on their personal goals. They'll be grateful for the growth, and will realize you care about them as people rather than just what you get from them. Other systems include wellness and savings programs you could implement, and perhaps quarterly seminars by outside experts on various aspects of personal development.

NOW WHAT?

Summary

Helping employees grow takes very little regular investment and intentionality, but produces outsized results in terms of employee loyalty, productivity, and maturity. It starts with being curious about your employees, paying attention to what is important to them, listening to how they want to grow, and supporting them as they pursue goals for personal growth. While much of this happens individually – especially with your leaders and potential leaders – there are some initiatives that can be programmed for all employees, such as wellness and savings plans. Beyond the "how-tos," many employees will need help pushing past mental and emotional barriers to growth. Build their confidence and help them see their own potential. Investing in employees is important because people matter, and is among your biggest opportunities to make a difference with your life.

Application Questions

1. How will you become more curious, attentive, supportive, and thoughtful?

2. How will you learn your employees' dreams? How will you help them come true?

3. How will you further develop yourself as a model for your employees?

4. When are the best opportunities in your work week to be more available to your employees?

5. Which high-potential employees will you help first?

6. What systems for personal goal setting, reviewing, and accountability will you encourage?

7. What resources will you use to help employees discover and pursue their potential, and overcome limiting mindsets?

8. Which experts will you bring in and how often?

Recommended Reading

Awaken the Giant Within by Anthony Robbins.

"Why Employee Development is Important, Neglected, and Can Cost You Talent" by Victor Limpman, Forbes, Jan 29th 2013:

http://www.forbes.com/sites/victorlipman/2013/01/29/why-development-planning-is-important-neglected-and-can-cost-you-young-talent/

Make it Happen!

What ideas has this chapter stirred in me?

What new light does this chapter shine on my leadership and my business?

What changes do I plan to make?

My actions to *Make it Happen!*	Completion dates	
	Proposed	Actual

Chapter 24 | Mentor Other Entrepreneurs

By Evan Keller

WHAT?

Definition

Business mentoring involves an ongoing, trusting relationship in which the mentor coaches, encourages, and supports the mentee in their business leadership. This is done through regular meetings in which the mentor listens, asks questions, offers advice, and encourages the mentee to set and achieve goals that lead to business growth and job creation.

Expert Quote

"Mentoring has become, for me, one of the chief duties of any leader" (Max De Pree, former CEO of Herman Miller, Leadership is an Art p.vii).

Assessment Questions

1. Who has been your best business advisor?

2. Do you enjoy passing on what you're learning in business?

3. Which of your business experiences and skills would be most valuable to a mentee?

WHY?

Benefits

Leverage. It is gratifying to know that your hard-earned lessons will help more than just your own enterprise.

Solidarity. Across industries and even cultures, entrepreneurs know what each other are going through. This can be a huge source of support when employees, family, and friends don't understand.

Growth. Mentors grow themselves since mentoring keeps them sharp in leading their own company.

Impact. The resulting business growth and job creation benefits entire communities.

Service. Most opportunities that entrepreneurs have to serve don't engage what they do best – grow businesses! Business mentoring is an opportunity to pass on your passion.

Barriers

Independence. Entrepreneurs are self-reliant; it's hard for some to admit they could use help.

Self-doubt. Potential mentors often doubt whether they have the right skills and experience to be effective. If you've started and grown a successful business, you've already done the hard part. Passing on that experience is easy.

Cross-cultural differences. There are language and culture barriers when mentoring internationally.

Suspicion. Building trust can be difficult when offering to mentor someone you don't know well. It may be difficult for your mentee to open up and share sensitive information, such as trade secrets, financials, conflicts, and failures.

Underlying Values

Service. We are most fulfilled when loving our "neighbor," which is central to our purpose as humans. – Mark 12:31

Relationships. As relational beings, we find meaning by connecting with others. – Genesis 2:18

Capacity Building. Entrepreneurs are eager to receive and pass on the high-impact investment of intellectual capital. As business know how is shared in the context of long-term friendships, local business leaders are cultivated and lead the way in addressing the needs of their communities.

Business as a force for good. As the primary mechanism for wealth creation, business is the best hope for creating dignity-enhancing jobs and lifting communities out of poverty. We believe this is central to the true purpose of business. – Deuteronomy 8:18

HOW?

Steps to Implement

<u>Establish the mentoring relationship(s):</u>

1. **Find two or three mentees to serve.** Offer to mentor someone with whom you already have mutual respect and trust.

2. **Choose mentees who are open to coaching and whose businesses have strong growth potential.** Make sure they are eager to pursue goals for personal and business growth.

3. **Create a trusting environment.** Promise strict confidentiality. Let mentees know they can expect you to listen with empathy and provide accountability and support for their work.

4. **Create structure together.** Agree on how often to meet, how long your meetings will be, and where you'll meet. (It's important to meet at least some of the time at your mentee's place of business.) Decide on whether to commit to one or two years.

5. **Set goals together.** Agree on goals for your mentoring relationship, such as growing their companies, creating jobs, and helping the community to thrive.

Know your role:

1. **Build relationships.** Making a personal connection is the environment in which the other objectives can flourish. Relationships are where transformation happens, so get acquainted and build trust.

2. **Coach business decisions.** Get to know their business, ask probing questions, and focus attention on aspects of the business where the greatest opportunities and challenges lie. Help them make better decisions and grow the business, leading towards a healthier culture and increased profitability.

3. **Mentor their leadership.** If you focus solely on "coaching business decisions", you could be accused of giving helpful advice without actually building their own capacity to make wiser decisions and become better business leaders. So, in addition to focusing on the business, focus on the leader of the business. This involves helping them grow personally and professionally in whatever ways will make them better leaders. This could be your most impactful investment.

4. **Make connections.** Isolation is one definition of poverty. We're all incredibly enriched by the connections we have in our community, so one of your key roles as a mentor is to facilitate connections between mentees and the people or resources which could add value to their businesses.

Follow mentoring best practices:

1. **Be a friend.** Show that you're more of a friend than a boss. Spend personal time with them and get to know their families.

2. **Encourage community service.** Help mentees to use their businesses to serve the community. Start by asking: "What community needs do you care about?" Help them turn their concerns into action, and look for ways you can work together to serve your community. Encourage community investment that is both intrinsic (through their goods, services, jobs and re-circulated revenue) and instrumental (through their relationships, time, influence and profits).

3. **Encourage integrity.** Help mentees build a culture of trust with their employees, customers and suppliers by consistently doing what they promise. Help them build teamwork that leads to win-win relationships.

4. **Face challenges together.** Share how you overcame the same obstacles they're facing, and be honest about the challenges that you still face. Don't pretend to have all the answers – mentees will relate to your weaknesses more than your strengths. Knowing you have struggles will help them face their own.

5. **Discuss their issues.** Allow mentees' current situation and felt needs to direct the conversation: "What would you like to discuss today?" Ask them early in each mentor visit what opportunities and challenges they're currently facing in their business.

6. **Ask thought-provoking questions.** Ask questions that help them think through important issues. Discovering the right direction will spur them to change more than being told what to do. "Good coaches ask open-ended questions that come from a non-expert position. They don't pretend to have the answers. If the client seems stuck, it may be appropriate to bring your answers into the conversation. If so, always present them in a generous rather than a judgmental framework" ("Art of Coaching" article by Vistage).

7. **Use *Grow*Book.** Discuss a chapter per month with your mentees, helping them apply it to their businesses.

8. **Use *Start*Book.** If they're in the startup phase, this curriculum of ours puts business in the simplest terms and action steps.

9. **Use the Big Picture.** This tool at the end of *Start*Book and *Grow*Book will help them assess their business strengths and weaknesses in a single minute.

10. **Use the Action Plan.** Help mentees assess the maturity of their businesses using the Action Plan at the end of *Grow*Book. It will help them decide which areas to work on over the next 12 months.

11. **Strategize the future.** Help mentees shift from just surviving today to creating a thriving future. Affirm their ability to improve their business, help them set long-term goals and work towards them step by step. Show how innovation and determination have improved your business over time.

12. **Offer advice.** Each time you meet, offer written recommendations which will improve their business.

13. **Encourage goal-setting.** At the end of each mentor visit, ask them to set and write down three goals to work on until you meet again. Ask how they did on those goals at your next meeting. Show respect for their ideas and affirm their ability to make positive changes.

14. **Keep your promises.** Write down and follow through on the ways you said you'd help them.

15. **Keep your appointments.** Schedule your next meeting, write it down, and remind them the day before. Be reliable and prompt to build trust and set a good example.

16. **Ask them to mentor others.** Encourage them to invest in two other entrepreneurs, keeping the coaching cascade going.

17. **Be positive.** Always find something in their work to compliment. Offer your listening ear, encouragement, prayer and support. Your affirming presence can make a big difference.

18. **Improve your mentoring skills.** Continue growing as a mentor by reflecting on your mentoring experiences and learning from reading and interacting with other mentors.

Case Study

Through the nonprofit I lead – Creating Jobs Inc – American business people have been mentoring groups of entrepreneurs in Haiti and Honduras since 2011 (and other countries since then). These relationships have been very rewarding and productive. We go for a week at a time and provide a business training seminar along with personalized mentoring in the mentees' businesses. For the first several years, our rotating team of mentors sent 1-3 mentors on quarterly visits, and now we go twice a year to support the mentees who have become mentors. They are taking the lead and making a difference in their communities. We've taken what we've learned from those years of mentoring developing-world entrepreneurs and created a certification training program. Through this Creating Jobs Academy, we equip global nonprofits to train entrepreneurs using our curricula (*Start*Book and *Grow*Book). If you want to learn more about using your training abilities and business acumen to serve with us, please email me at: evan@creatingjobs.org and check out our programs at creatingjobs.org.

Here is rough outline of what an individualized mentoring session looks like in our international programs:

Exchange warm greetings in their own language.

Find a quiet place to sit, if possible.

Ask and share about families.

Ask and share about business.

Share any resources you researched for them.

Ask "How did you do towards accomplishing your goals for the last three months?"

Ask "What would you like to discuss today?"

Along with your own questions to spur growth in their leadership and their business, use the Business Health Profile to discuss issues they are facing.

Analyze their latest financial reports together.

Record current job count.

Offer your top three recommendations and ask them to write their top three goals for the next three months.

Record them yourself and follow up on their progress. Let them know when to expect a follow up visit and also when you will return.

Discuss at least one aspect of helping him or her become a mentor, such as: the importance of mentoring, their ability and progress towards becoming a mentor, a simple process to begin, or the challenges and opportunities of the entrepreneurs they're mentoring.

Discuss ways they can leverage their business to serve the community.

Invite them to the business training events, if available.

End with affirmation of the positive things you're seeing in their business and pray for them if they would like.

Leading Self, Employees, Systems

SELF – Since you're used to being "the boss," it takes an adjustment to share advice and push them a little while also affirming that the decisions are theirs to make. Listening actively and asking through-provoking questions are important skills to grow in.

EMPLOYEES – While your employees likely won't have a role in this, it may be positive for them to know that you're giving back. In some cases, you might even mentor an employee who aspires to start a business. While non-compete clauses and caution with your trade secrets are often wise, entrepreneurs can be overly fearful of competitors. Having strong competitors can be positive, and if your business is providing exceptional value, you shouldn't fear a startup. I'm proud to see several former employees succeeding in their own businesses in the same industry.

SYSTEMS – Creating Jobs Inc has a variety of free tools to help you be an effective mentor. The most important process is to update your written mentor recommendations and their mentee goals each time you meet. Use these to shape your conversations and accountability.

NOW WHAT?

Summary

Business mentors must apply their people skills and business skills to be effective in helping both the mentees and their businesses grow. After finding coachable mentees who are eager to improve their leadership and their businesses, you'll need to develop personal, mutually beneficial relationships of trust with them. Through your questions, advice, encouragement, and accountability, help them set and achieve goals, grow their businesses, create jobs, and leverage their businesses to serve their communities.

Application Questions

1. Do you want to try business mentoring? If so, who are some potential mentees?
2. Would you rather mentor on your own or work with Creating Jobs Inc?
3. What hesitations do you have, if any, about your readiness to serve as a business mentor?

4. How good are you at crafting and asking open-ended questions that will help your mentees discover solutions to their challenges?

5. Which of the above best practices will be the most challenging for you?

Recommended Reading

"Art of Coaching" article by Vistage

Make it Happen!

What ideas has this chapter stirred in me?

What new light does this chapter shine on my leadership and my business?

What changes do I plan to make?

My actions to *Make it Happen!*	Completion dates	
	Proposed	Actual

Chapter 25 | Serve with Time, Talent & Treasure

By Evan Keller

WHAT?

Definition

While some see it as an obligation, it is actually a joy to serve the community and world with the time, talent, and treasure you are entrusted with. You have profits, skills, and energy that can make unique contributions to improving our world. In addition to being fulfilling, it makes your business more attractive to customers.

Expert Quote

"Entrepreneurs invent, create, envision the future, produce things, feed people, save lives, and enhance others' well-being by risking their money and time" (The Poverty of Nations by Wayne Grudem and Barry Asmus p.179).

Assessment Questions

1. What is your current level of serving with time, talent, and treasure?

2. Is it at the right level given the profitability of your business?

3. What is the moment of generosity you're most proud of?

WHY?

Benefits

Fulfilment. We're happiest when serving others.

Attraction. Customers and employees want to work with people who show that they care.

Leverage. The years of back-breaking effort to launch your business made you a stronger and smarter person. Now those hard-earned lessons can pay off for more than just your own venture. They can benefit the nonprofit world.

Barriers

Single bottom line. If you only value profit, you won't be very motivated to serve.

Lack of leaders and systems. If your business is not mature, it will depend on you constantly – like an infant with its mother – preventing you from significant outside service. See chapter 13.

Cash flow problems. If you're still struggling to make weekly payroll, you may not be able to contribute much financially to causes you care about. Likewise, your time and talent maybe focused only on making necessary business improvements. See chapter 16.

Underlying Values

Empowerment. We should build capacity of the under-poor with the tools to better themselves.

Generosity. The giver always seems to receive as much as the recipient. – 2 Corinthians 9:6-11

Love. "Love your neighbor as yourself." – Mark 12:31

Hope. We are motivated by confidence that our service matters and makes a difference. – Proverbs 11:10-11

Stewardship. We are responsible to wisely use what we've been given. – Mathew 25:20-21

HOW?

Steps to Implement

Examine your mindset. Do you really believe that you can make a difference? Or is this world too broken – with poverty, injustice, and violence being so entrenched and beyond rooting out? Without resorting to a belief that we humans will fix this broken world on our own, do you believe God will make all things right and beautiful someday that even your tiniest efforts for good really matter? If so, that sense of hopefulness is one of the strongest possible motivations to give your wholehearted effort to making the world a better place.

Grow your economic engine. Without a strong business, you won't have the time or money to give to community organizations. A strong business will also increase your respect within the community. This added influence will allow you to get more done and bring more people alongside you to serve – if you choose to use it in that way.

Sharpen your skills. As you develop a mature business, you'll master some amazing skills that can be used in a variety of ways to serve the world.

See business as a force for good. When first starting my business, I was really surprised at all the new opportunities it opened up to make a difference. While charity is often based on handouts that perpetuate dependence, business is by definition the most sustainable vehicle on the planet! And although business has been used as a tool of greed to exploit people and environments, its true purpose is to serve communities with jobs that enhance their dignity and products/services that meet their physical needs.

Realize how much you have to offer. A powerful combination for leveraging business for good is your economic engine, business acumen, and hopeful outlook. Refer to my diagram at the end of the chapter to see how lacking any of these three reduces your ability to serve optimally with your time, talent, and treasure. But these three together give you to the: heart to give, way to give, and value to give. This is a rare and powerful combination; don't squander it.

Serve with your top skills. Business talents are often wasted when business people are asked to do things that almost anyone could do.

Use your actual products and services to improve the world. Hopefully, the sale of your products are already meeting real needs. Are there situations where you can do more – such as discounting your products for nonprofits you trust? Perhaps you could contribute products to serve those who've lost everything in an accident or natural disaster. Or maybe an employee's friend or family member has a special need your services can meet; this would deepen your employee engagement while serving those in need.

Improve your industry. Mostly by your company's example, force your competitors to improve to stay in business. Teaming up with others, you can also improve expectations or regulations for companies in your industry. Everybody wins – especially the customer.

Consider serving with Creating Jobs Inc. We offer you the opportunity to use your business skills for the global good. You can help us "co-create thriving businesses and communities." You'd be surprised at how almost everything you've learned and endured in your own business can help someone else in theirs – even in a vastly different culture. Instead of giving handouts which undercut initiative, we build capacity of entrepreneurs to meet the needs of their own communities. It's thrilling to see courageous entrepreneurs respond to your one-to-one mentoring and business seminars with positive changes in their businesses that reduce poverty in their communities. The ongoing friendships are equally fulfilling. See how our programs work at www.creatingjobs.org and drop me a line if you have any questions: evan@creatingjobs.org.

Find your focus. Whether it's with Creating Jobs Inc or another organization, we suggest funnelling your time, talent, and treasure into one or two rivers rather than a dozen small streams. This will optimize your effectiveness. While I volunteer a little with my Rotary Club, most of my focus goes to running Creating Jobs Inc. Donating my time for that is even written into the operating agreement of Tree Work Now Inc.

Involve your employees. Some companies build their entire culture around community service, paying and recognizing employees for their volunteer hours. For example, Frontier Communications involves hundreds of employees at every level in volunteerism. It is a major sense of team work, company pride, and employee engagement. You could also get employee input on which nonprofits you donate to. (Be prepared to hear: "I'm a charity!") We've found this is very engaging for some employees. Another approach is to match a percentage of employees' own donations to charities of their choice.

Involve your customers. People feel good about doing business with socially conscious businesses. "For every pair of glasses Warby Parker sells, it makes a donation that enables optical training in developing countries....By rooting the brand in something meaningful, Warby Parker passes on that meaning to its consumers, making them feel empowered by a purchase that not only looks amazing without breaking the bank, but also contributes to the greater good" (Hamish Campbell, Entrepreneur Magazine, August 2015, p.46).

Decide how you want to give money. At Tree Work Now, our target is to donate 10% of what we're able to add to long-term savings. This motivates us to save and ensures that our giving doesn't cripple our cash flow.

Decide who to give money to. Our criteria at Tree Work Now are:

1. **Focus.** We'd rather give larger gifts to a few organizations for bigger impact. 1/3 of our giving goes to Creating Jobs Inc.

2. **Need.** All nonprofits have ongoing needs, but disasters create special needs. I leveraged a gift from Tree Work Now to involve my Rotary Club's board and members in giving $1150 to the families of the Charleston shooting victims.

3. **Effectiveness.** Nonprofits are geared to address systemic, long-term needs, but vary widely in their effectiveness. Look for strong results.

4. **Relationship.** It makes sense to give where there's a personal connection. Donations strengthen those relationships and open up other ways to give.

5. **Values.** We give to organizations with whom we have some common values.

Case Study

Rajesh, an immigrant from India resides with his beautiful family in Lake Helen, FL and works as a software designer. I had been looking for an opportunity to use Tree Work Now Inc to somehow serve villagers in the poor village of La Salle, Haiti, where they had to walk to the next village for fresh water. As I presented my estimate to Rajesh for the day's worth of tree work his property needed, I realized that *this* was my moment. He showed considerable interest when he learned that we did international development work. So we worked it out so that his donation would fund the project that was needed in Haiti: my crew would perform his tree work at no cost to him, and he would write a $2,000 check that would go towards drilling a well in that waterless Haitian village. This creative forging of relationships and use of resources was quite satisfying. While my company received no payment for an entire day's use of my heavy equipment and large crew's labor, it was perhaps our best day yet! As my employees sweated that day, they knew their efforts were serving fellow humans trapped in chronic poverty in a difficult economic environment, perhaps sparking a desire to continue doing so. They were somewhat confounded that I was paying them while not being paid myself. All parties involved did their part for the global good that day. What a day it was.

Leading Self, Employees, Systems

SELF – You may need to invest in yourself (skills and company growth) before you can give as much as you'd like. Don't sink your business in your eagerness to give. You can actually do more in the long run by building a strong business. Caveat: that doesn't mean you can't start small now. There's value in building the discipline and virtue of generosity.

EMPLOYEES – The best way to lead your team is by example. Employees will see that you're not ruled by greed; that you're not only a boss – you're a human with a heart.

SYSTEMS – The principled giving we suggest above helps you to decide in advance what types of needs you'll address. The same approach can apply to your time; *others* will fill up your schedule with their priorities if *you* don't first. (See chapter 1.) A system for employees would be to compensate for some of their volunteer hours. A system for customers would be a buy-one-give-one program such as used by Tom's Shoes or giving a percentage of profits to a particular cause.

NOW WHAT?

Summary

Business can be a powerful force for good in the community and world. An entrepreneur with a strong business engine, solid business skills, and a hopeful outlook is brimming with potential impact. Focus your time and talent in a single direction to make the biggest difference. You can also give funds in a systematic and purposeful way.

Recipe: Business for Good

Application Questions

1. What is your strongest motivation for making a difference in the world?

2. What are your personal strengths and passions and how do they intersect the greatest needs in your community?

3. What community need is your business uniquely positioned to meet?

4. How might your employees want to volunteer? How can you empower them to do so and build teamwork in the process?

5. How can you involve your customers in serving the greater good?

6. Are you interested becoming a business mentor with Creating Jobs Inc?

7. What process and parameters for giving funds best fits your company?

Recommended Reading

Start Something That Matters by Blake Mycoskie

The Poverty of Nations by Wayne Grudem and Barry Asmus

Make it Happen!

What ideas has this chapter stirred in me?

What new light does this chapter shine on my leadership and my business?

What changes do I plan to make?

My actions to *Make it Happen!*	Completion dates	
	Proposed	Actual

Circle the appropriate action for each topic:

Giving Back

23. **Help Employees Grow** - *Am I intentionally helping employees to grow their skills, maximize their strengths, and reach their aspirations?*

        Maintain   Fine-Tune   Overhaul

24. **Mentor Other Entrepreneurs** - *Am I building trusting relationships with teachable entrepreneurs, offering thought-provoking questions, regular encouragement, and sound advice? Do I help them set and achieve goals for business growth and job creation?*

        Maintain   Fine-Tune   Overhaul

25. **Serve with Time, Talent & Treasure** - *Am I leveraging my business and influence to serve my community? Do I use my profits and skills to make a difference in the world?*

        Maintain   Fine-Tune   Overhaul

MY #1 FOCUS: _____

Conclusion

By Evan Keller

Most of this book is only common sense, so the real value is putting it into practice. The biggest shift towards maturing your business comes by spending more time working "on" it rather than "in" it. Just like lifting weights may seem like a waste of time today, leaving you sore and weak, it builds muscle for tomorrow. It's all about building capacity. Let's switch the metaphor to parenting. If you shelter your child for 20 years from all decisions and dangers, can you expect her to make stellar decisions the first day she is on her own? If a good parenting strategy is to give ever-increasing responsibility with real consequences, then I ask "Is your business mature enough to survive without you?" Not that you want to leave it, but you may want an adult-to-adult relationship with it. When you no longer have to change its diapers, you can have a more enjoyable and mutual relationship.

And a successful business isn't always enormous. It's better to be healthy than huge. "It's easy to confuse size with greatness and getting bigger with getting better" (Burlingham p.257).

Revenue growth is often needed, but there are more important ways to grow, including: efficiency, excellence, employee engagement, cash position, and customer satisfaction. We hope you take the advice in this book to mature your business, with help from the Action Plan and Make it Happen planning tools in this book. Best of all, you'll grow personally as you practice good leadership and serve your community.

Once you've built a thriving business, we hope you'll consider using your skillset as a business trainer or mentor with Creating Jobs Inc. Learn about our programs at creatingjobs.org or email us at info@creatingjobs.org. We'd love to hear your ideas to make this book better for other entrepreneurs. Thanks for reading!

GrowBook Snapshot

GrowBook offers 25 steps to mature your business to operate smoothly and profitably – even when you're not present. It all starts with you setting goals to improve yourself and your business constantly, then taking steady action...

Build a brand that centers on customer needs. Find a solution that customers crave and "wow" them every time. Give top-priority effort to turning that trust into a steady flow of new customers. To efficiently produce what your customers want, build a team of thriving employees who: share your values, have real responsibility, enjoy strong teamwork, and keep honing their skills. Give them a clear path to develop within your company. With your employees' help, build systems they can use to produce reliable and efficient results. Be frugal with spending and diligent with saving to patiently build financial strength. Use your expanding resources, acumen and influence to serve others.

The key pivot to putting GrowBook into practice is working less "in" your business and more "on" your business. Transition from being a great technician to a successful entrepreneur.

GrowBook At-a-Glance

Figure out who you are and where you're going as a person and as a business. Improve yourself and your business every day, using reading, thinking, writing and acting as primary tools.

Center your marketing messages on customer needs. Until you have more customers than you can serve, make it your number one priority to find them online and face-to-face.

Provide solutions that customers crave and use customer feedback to improve them. Work to produce with ever-increasing efficiency.

Sell at a high margin based on trust and superior value. Reinforce both by exceeding customer expectations.

Multiply your capacity by raising up leaders with real authority. Create a win-win by helping employees grow their skills and build their teamwork. Show them a path for advancement, and that you care.

Steadily build wealth by being: vigilant in managing cash, diligent in saving, frugal with spending, strategic in negotiating, cautious with borrowing, and careful in protecting your business.

Use all you've been given to benefit others – serving employees, entrepreneurs, community and world. Therein your time, talent and treasure will find their true purpose and joy.

What does each aspect of my business need?
Write "maintain", "fine-tune", or "overhaul" under each icon.

My BiG Focus:

472

PONDER these 25 questions to assess your growth towards each accomplishment.

CIRCLE "maintain", "fine-tune", or "overhaul" to identify your business needs over the next 12 months.

Part One | Leadership

1. **Lead Yourself** - *Are you intentionally investing in your personal relationships, growth, and health?*

        Maintain   Fine-Tune   Overhaul

2. **Set the Course** - *Have you written your company vision, mission, and values? Do you ensure everything else aligns with them?*

        Maintain   Fine-Tune   Overhaul

3. **Pursue Goals** - *Have you written goals for this year and do you faithfully pursue them?*

        Maintain   Fine-Tune   Overhaul

4. **Develop Systems** - *Do you write, implement, and improve employee processes to increase efficiency in your operations and consistency to your customers?*

Maintain　　　Fine-Tune　　　Overhaul

5. **Innovate Constantly** - *Are you always finding ways to improve your business?*

Maintain　　　Fine-Tune　　　Overhaul

6. **Overcome Fatalism** - *Do you believe the truth that you are empowered to positively shape your future?*

Maintain　　　Fine-Tune　　　Overhaul

Part Two | **Market Position**

7. **Craft Customer-Focused Branding** - *Have you developed a name, tagline, and logo that speaks to your customers' needs and reveals your unique solutions?*

Maintain　　　Fine-Tune　　　Overhaul

8. **Generate a Sufficient Flow of Customers** - *Do you have a strong lead generation system? If not, are you spending considerable time pursuing potential customers?*

Maintain　　　Fine-Tune　　　Overhaul

Part Three | **Production**

9. **Create Unique Customer Solutions** - *Do you provide unique solutions that people want and fit with your company identity? Do you make prototypes of new products and test them with some of your customers?*

        Maintain   Fine-Tune   Overhaul

10. **Produce Efficiently** - *Are you working to improve the efficiency of your production so that you can please customers better and faster?*

        Maintain   Fine-Tune   Overhaul

Part Four | **Sales & Service**

11. **Close Sufficient High-Margin Sales** - *Do you build trusting relationships with your potential customers, communicating the value you offer and standing firm on your prices?*

        Maintain   Fine-Tune   Overhaul

12. **Multiply Happy Customers** - *Do you consistently exceed your customers' expectations and go beyond what is required to fix your customer mistakes?*

        Maintain   Fine-Tune   Overhaul

Part Five | **Employees**

13. Develop Sales, Production & Office Leaders - *Have you been able to let go of these areas of responsibility and empower others to excel in them?*

        Maintain   Fine-Tune   Overhaul

14. Engage Employees - *Have you built a positive company culture so that employees care about the company and their work?*

        Maintain   Fine-Tune   Overhaul

15. Build Teamwork - *Are you developing team members and the team as a whole, helping them work together to achieve clear goals that align with your values?*

        Maintain   Fine-Tune   Overhaul

Part Six | **Finance**

16. Achieve Positive Cash Flow - *Are you practicing effective cash flow management, building systems to prevent future cash flow crises?*

        Maintain   Fine-Tune   Overhaul

17. **Save Money Regularly** - *Are you regularly saving as much as you can in a separate account, patiently building financial strength?*

        Maintain   Fine-Tune   Overhaul

18. **Control Spending Closely** - *Are you becoming more efficient by tracking your expenses and monitoring employee purchases?*

        Maintain   Fine-Tune   Overhaul

19. **Negotiate Good Deals** - *Do you negotiate great deals by learning what is important to the other party, building trust, and seeking to achieve your top priorities while meeting some of theirs?*

        Maintain   Fine-Tune   Overhaul

20. **Access Capital & Limit Debt** - *Are you gaining access to capital by being profitable, controlling debt, and providing documentation to lenders? Do you avoid unnecessary loans and pay down your loans as quickly as possible?*

        Maintain   Fine-Tune   Overhaul

21. **Manage Major Risks** - *Have you identified and managed your major risks related to property, employees, and customers?*

        Maintain   Fine-Tune   Overhaul

22. **Resist Corruption** - *Have you written policies and*

procedures so your employees know how to respond to unethical demands? Do you resist corruption even when it's costly?

        Maintain   Fine-Tune   Overhaul

Part Seven | Giving Back

23. Help Employees Grow - *Are you intentionally helping employees grow their skills, maximize their strengths, and reach their aspirations?*

        Maintain   Fine-Tune   Overhaul

24. Mentor Other Entrepreneurs - *Are you building trusting relationships with teachable entrepreneurs, offering thought-provoking questions, regular encouragement, and sound advice? Do you help them set and achieve goals for business growth and job creation?*

        Maintain   Fine-Tune   Overhaul

25. Serve with Time, Talent & Treasure - *Are you leveraging your business and influence to serve your community? Do you use your profits and skills to make a difference in the world?*

        Maintain   Fine-Tune   Overhaul

Action Plan Summary

Number of areas to...	My top three areas of strength:
Maintain: _____	1. _____
Fine-Tune: _____	2. _____
Overhaul: _____	3. _____

Top three areas I'll act on: And my next step for each:

1._____
_____

2._____
_____

3._____
_____

CreatingJobs.org
Business for Global Good

480

Contributors

Evan Keller, Lead Author & General Editor – Evan is married to his beloved wife Karen of 26 years – a former nurse who's an awesome cook and baker. In addition to escaping to the mountains, they enjoy their life together in Central Florida, which is near to their super-fun 13 nieces and nephews! Evan is addicted to playing basketball and mountain backpacking, and dabbles in off-road biking and paddling. He appreciates close friends, crossing cultures, art, blues music, and books on theology and business. At work, he's the Founder/Executive Director of Creating Jobs Inc & Founder/CEO of Tree Work Now Inc.

Jennifer Pettie, Author – "Jen" owns a real estate business in Burlington, North Carolina where she is an accountant with 10 years of experience in finance and audit. She enjoys running in races and entertaining her dog Artie, who wishes she would let him sleep on the sofa. (Otherwise he thinks she is wonderful and gives the best treats.) She's pursuing an advanced degree in data science and is a Lead Mentor with Creating Jobs Inc in Haiti.

Mano De La Vega, Author – Mano is a Mexican-American married to Venezeulan-American Janett, with children Mia and Diego. Together, they make a beautiful, smart, and fun family. Mano has a background in engineering and is Founder/CEO of De La Vega Restaurante & Galleria along with his sister, Chef Nora. They feature fine Central Mexican cuisine and a unique, close-knit employee culture. See delavegart.com. Mano is the Lead Mentor for Creating Jobs Inc in Mexico and has been a big part of shaping and growing the organization.

Grace John, Author – Grace is an Indian-American who migrated to Ft. Lauderdale, Florida at a young age. Her leadership approach and core values were fostered by Indian immigrant parents with Christian values. She enjoys running, traveling especially locations that have great spas! and spending time with family – especially her two young nephews!

Grace is a Senior Director at a Fortune 200 energy company and serves as a Board Member of Creating Jobs Inc.

Dr. Carol Keller-Vlangas – Bibliography creator, proof-reader, and Evan's mom.

Karen Keller – Proof-reader, source of great ideas, and Evan's wife.

Paris Pena – Videographer for GrowBook's indiegogo.com campaign, paris@volusia.me.

Neal Aspinall – Icon artist, NealAspinall.com.

E-Book Launch – Formatting of e-book, team@ebooklaunch.com.

Donors – Paulette Boyer, Blair Brumenschenkel, Andrew Hardesty, and Jeff Hostetter. Thanks very much!

 **Cross Lingo - Jose Elvir**, Translator (Spanish), facebook.com/crosslingo.

 Colibri Translation Services - John Adams, Translator (French, Haitian Creole), colibritranslation@gmail.com.

 **Polgarus Studio** – Formatting of print book, www.polgarusstudio.com.

 Partners Worldwide – We've learned a lot from you and enjoy working alongside you to serve developing-world entrepreneurs. Thank you for your partnership.

 **Tree Work Now Inc** - A big thanks to my brother and business partner, Dani Keller, and our great team at Tree Work Now Inc. By skillfully filling some of my former roles, they empower the work of Creating Jobs Inc – including this book.

 **Creating Jobs Inc** – Its board members, mentors, trainers and inspiring entrepreneurs are weaved into the fabric of this book. A heart felt thank you to all!

Bibliography

12-questions-to-measure-employee-engagement. (n.d.). Retrieved from Gallup's Employee Engagement Survey: (http://www.dandbconsulting.com/12-questions-to-measure-employee-engagement).

5-employee-engagement-activities-to-help-your-bottom-line. (n.d.). Retrieved from Frontstream blog: Frontstream blog: (http://www.frontstream.com/5-employee-engagement-activities-to-help-your-bottom-line).

Andruss, P. (2012, April). *Secrets of the 10 Most-Trusted Brands.* Retrieved from Entrepreneur Magazine: (http://www.entrepreneur.com/article/223125).

Blanchard Training and Development, Inc. (n.d.). *Creating Effective Leaders Through Situational Leadership.* Retrieved from Blanchard Training and Development: (https://www.theseus.fi/bitstream/handle/10024/33027/Mwai_Esther.pdf?sequence=2)

BIBLIOGRAPHY

Bluestein, A. (2013, September). You're Not That Innovative. *INC Magazine.*

Bowles, S. (2009, March). *When Economic Incentives Backfire.* Retrieved from HBR.org: (https://hbr.org/2009/03/when-economic-incentives-backfire).

Brodsky, N., & Burlington, B. (2008). *Street Smarts.* New York: Portfolio Hardcover.

Buckingham, & Coffman. (1999). New York: Simon and Schuster.

Burlingham, B. (2016). *Small Giants.* New York: Penguin.

Campbell, H. (2015, August). *Entrepreneur Magazine*, p. 46.

Clark, R. P. (2008). *Writing Tools.* New York: Little, Brown, and Co.

Collins, J. (2011). *Good to Great.* New York: Harper Collins.

Collins, J. (2012, June). From Good to Great. *INC Magazine*, p. 71.

Covey, S. (1989). *The Seven Habits of Highly Effective People.* New York: Simon and Schuster.

Crouch, A. (2008). *Culture Making.* Downers Grove: Intervarsity Press.

Cunningham, M., & Clifton, D. (2001). *Now, Discover Your Strengths.* New York: The Free Press.

DenBesten, K. (2008). *Shine.* Shippensburg: Destiny Image.

DePree, M. (2004). *Leadership as Art.* New York: DoubleDay.

Employee-engagement-ideas-that-work. (n.d.). Retrieved from Truist blog: (http://truist.com/employee-engagement-ideas-that-work).

Eurich, T. (2014, May). Bankable Leadership. *Entrepreneur Magazine.*

Flatworld Knowledge. (n.d.). Retrieved from Bookhub: (http://catalog.flatworldknowledge.com/bookhub/7?e=collins-ch11_s03).

Ford, H. (n.d.). *Quotes of Authors.* Retrieved from Brain Quote.com:

(http://www.brainyquote.com/quotes/authors/h/henry_ford.html).

Fried, J. (2011, February). How to Turn Disaster into Gold. *Inc Magazine.*

Frisch, B. (2011). *Harvard Business Review on Building Better Teams.* Boston: Harvard Business Review Press.

George, M. (2004). *The Lean Six Sigma Pocket Toolbook.* New York: McGraw Hill.

Gerber, M. (2005). *E-Myth Mastery.* New York: Harper Collins.

Greger, M. (2015). *How Not to Die.* New York: Flatiron Books.

Grudem, W., & Asmus, B. (2013). *The Poverty of Nations.* Wheaton: Crossing Books.

Harnish, V. (2014). *Scaling Up.* Ashburn, VA: Gazelles, Inc.

Heath, C., & Heath, D. (2008). *Made to Stick.* New York: Random House.

Hirshberg, M. C. (2012, December). *Let's Talk About This.* Retrieved from INC Magazine:

(http://www.inc.com/magazine/201212/meg-cadoux-hirshberg/lets-talk-about-this.html).

Hock, D. (2002, Winter). The Art of Chaordic Leadership. *Leader to Leader*, p. 22.

How a Small Business Can Use Lean Manufacturing. (n.d.). Retrieved from Mike on Manufacturing: (http://www.mikeonmanufacturing.com/mike-on-manufacturing/2009/12/how-a-small-business-can-use-lean-manufacturing.html).

Hybels, B. (2002). *Courageous Leadership.* Grand Rapids: Zondervan.

Karol, R., & Nelson, B. (n.d.). *New Product Development for Dummies.*

Kahle, D. (2017, April). *Finding the Right Business Model or Being the Right Business Leader?* Retrieved from the Business as Mission Blog: (http://businessasmission.com/models-or-leaders-staff-pick/).

Kotter, J. (1996). *Leading Change.* Boston: Harvard Review.

Kruse, K. (2012, June 22). *Employee Engagement 2.0.* Retrieved from Forbes.com: (http://www.forbes.com/sites/kevinkruse/2012/06/22/employee-engagement-what-and-why/).

Lapin, D. (2002). *Thou Shall Prosper.* Hoboken: John, Wiley, and Sons, Inc.

Lausanne Movement. (2017, October 18). *Wealth Creation: Biblical Views and Perspectives.* Retrieved from Lausanne.org: (https://www.lausanne.org/content/wealth-creation-biblical-views-perspectives)

Lencioni, P. (2002). *The Five Dysfunctions of a Team.* San Francisco: Jossey Bass.

Lewis, C. S. (2001). *The Weight of Glory.* New York: Harper One.

Limpman, V. (2013, January 29). *Why Employee Development Is Important, Neglected And Can Cost You Talent.* Forbes.

Manoj, J. (2013). *Risk Management for Small Businesses.* Create Space.

Manoj, J. (2015, July 24). *Risk Management for Small Businesses.* Retrieved from Small Business Risk Management Resources from SMDC: (www2.lsbdc.org/Documentmaster.aspx?doc=2313).

Marquet, D. (2012). *Turn the Ship Around.* New York: Penguin.

Medina, J. (2014). *Brain Rules.* Seattle: Pear Press.

Meuteman, R. (2014, May). *Entrepreneur Magazine.*

Miller, M. (2015). *Chess Not Checkers.* Oakland, CA: Berrett-Koehler Publishers, Inc.

Mullainathan, S. (2013, December 17). *Why is Saving Money So Hard?* Retrieved from Time Magazine: (http://time.com/money/671/why-is-saving-money-so-hard/).

Munger, T. T. (2014, April 30). *Quote #51.* Retrieved from Top-100-money-quotes-of-all-time: T.T. Munger: (http://www.forbes.com/sites/robertberger/2014/04/30/top-100-money-quotes-of-all-time), quote # 51.

Mycoskie, B. (2011). *Start Something that Matters.* New York: Spiegel & Grau.

Nussbaum, S. (2005). *American Cultural Baggage*. Maryknoll: Orbis Books.

Pink, D. H. (2010). *Drive: The Surprising Truth About What Motivates Us*. Penguin Audio.

Ramieri, J., & Ramieri, M. (n.d.). *Buyer's Guide*. Retrieved from Inspired Bronze.com: (www.inspiredbronze.com).

Ramsey, D. (2011). *Entreleadership*. New York: Howard Books.

Ranking Factors. (2012, July 24). Retrieved from moz.com: (https://moz.com/local-search-ranking-factors).

Robbins, A. (2007). *Awaken the Giant Within*. New York: Free Press.

Robinson, J. (2013, May). *Entrepreneur Magazine*, p. 64.

SMART Goals. (2015, July 24). Retrieved from Wikipedia: (www.wikipedia.org/wiki/SMART_criteria).

Stanley, A. (2007). *Making Vision Stick*. Grand Rapids: Zondervan.

Starting Manufacturing Business Guide. (n.d.). Retrieved from Bizfilings.com: (http://www.bizfilings.com/Libraries/pdfs/starting-manufacturing-business-guide.sflb.ashx).

Warrell, M. (2017, May 30). Pursue Purpose Over Success: The Science Behind Mark Zuckerberg's Advice to Harvard Grads Retrieved from Forbes.com: (https://www.forbes.com/sites/margiewarrell/2017/05/30/feeling-stuck-take-zuckerbergs-advice-and-commit-to-a-purpose-bigger-than-yourself/#14731db7462e)

Wickman, G. (2011). *Traction.* Dallas, TX: BenBella Books.

Younker, J. (2000). *The Art of Coaching.* SanDiego: Vistage International.

Ziglar, Z. (2004). *Secrets of Closing the Sale.* Grand Rapids: Revell.

Made in the USA
Columbia, SC
09 June 2020